CLOSE TO THE EARTH

HAVE YOUR GARDEN
AND EAT IT TOO

Canadian Cataloguing in Publication Data

Mallory, Enid, 1938–
    Close to the Earth: Have Your Garden And Eat It Too

Includes bibliographical references and index.

ISBN 0-9693497-4-2

1. Vegetable gardening. 2. Organic gardening. 3. Cookery (Vegetables).
 I. Title.

SB324.3.M34 1998   635   C98-930796-4

Jacket front: Garden at Lily Lake in July.

Jacket back: Red wagon and vegetable harvest.

Facing page: Levern Wood's garden in August.

Published by Peterborough Publishing
(a division of Mallpro Corporation)
R.R.#2, Peterborough, Ontario, K9J 6X3

Printed and bound in Canada.

CLOSE TO THE EARTH

HAVE YOUR GARDEN
AND EAT IT TOO

ENID MALLORY

PHOTOGRAPHY: ENID AND GORD MALLORY

ACKNOWLEDGEMENTS

Nobody gardens alone. Whoever digs in the earth belongs to a large fraternity that knows no geographical bounds. Garden magazines and media programs inspire us with what some gardener in Peru or Alaska is doing.

Closer to home we have the more practical advice of those who share the same landscape and the same climate zone, the neighbour next door, the friend with a farm, the kindred souls in a garden group. For this book countless people answered questions, shared knowledge, seeds, plants, recipes or stories.

A special thanks to Mary Perlmutter for first telling us what organic gardening was all about; to Cathy Dueck whose work at the Peterborough Ecology Garden has inspired gardeners locally and far afield; to Arlene Stephens who starts thousands of seeds growing every spring and shares them far and wide; to Levern Wood who gets up at 4:00 or 5:00 a.m. to banish every weed from his garden before the rest of us get up, who supplies the water for our garden from a pump in Lily Lake and has a solution for every outdoor problem; to Irene Beer who taught me about staying 'grounded' through yoga practice; to everyone in our gardening group who can get excited about vegetables in January and wildflowers in February.

Among others who contributed in some way are Linda Fierheller, Bob Fitts, Joan Mercer, Mitchell Hewson, Irvine Lywood, Joan Rawlinson, Bob and Irene Williamson, Pat Rattenbury, Ethel Roe, Joan and John Smith, Tina Staplin, Dr. Diana Beresford-Kroeger, and Kim Naish.

A special thanks to Gord Mallory for long hours in the computer dungeon and to Jean Brien, our editor.

Photo Credits
pages 6 and 49, Jonathan Mallory;
pages 11 and 56, Joan Mercer, YWCA;
page 105, Bob Williamson;
page 106, Irene Williamson;
all others, Enid and Gord Mallory.

Disclaimer
Any application of information in this book is at the reader's discretion and sole responsibility.

for anyone who gardens
(especially Garden Group 3)

Good Stuff!

TABLE OF CONTENTS

Digging carrots at
Hillview Farm, Warsaw,
Ontario.

INTRODUCTION

Gardening is like creating the world. Since we are not God we cannot do it in seven days but we can feel the satisfaction of taking a bare piece of earth in April and saying, "Let there be plants growing lush and tall by July and let the people who live here eat the fruits of the earth all year". The thrill of gardening is the wonder of creation.

There are practical, less romantic reasons for planting a garden. It is cheaper than golf or tennis. It is an exercise club with no membership fee. It lets you eat well all year without pesticides in your food. It fills your freezer or larder with foodstuffs which are not over-packaged and do not have to be carted home from a store.

Catharine Parr Traill knew what it was like to be a long way from the "store". At age 32 she was transplanted from a large English country home where gardeners and servants supplied her wants, to a backwoods cabin near Peterborough where she alone sometimes stood between her children and starvation. In the preface of her *Canadian Crusoes,* 1850, her sister Agnes Strickland describes Canada as a country "...where no one need beg, and where any one may dig without being ashamed."[1]

Catharine learned from the Ojibwa which wild plants to eat and how to grow Indian corn; she experimented each year with seeds sent from home or given to her by settler neighbours. She was in her nineties when she sat down and wrote the accumulated lore of a lifetime in her *Studies of Plant Life in Canada.*

Most of us have grown up too close to the store and have lost or temporarily shelved much of the knowledge our ancestors had of working with the earth to grow good things. But there is evidence that we are re-learning the skills. A century after Catharine wrote her *Plant Life*, gardening is big in Canada. Industry sales have doubled in the last decade. The accumulated power of millions of people each planting a garden or a tree, is momentous.

Just by being there a garden enhances the earth and improves the world. All things green and growing contribute to the atmosphere we breathe. Then there's the visual joy of a well-kept garden, the colour of the flowers, the texture of the foliage and the fragrance of the herbs which promote a sense of well-being.

Meanwhile the garden will supply family and friends with good taste, all the vitamins we need and superb freshness from vegetables picked or pulled, cooked and served, all within thirty minutes.

The purpose of this book is to make our ground connection a little stronger, to use and enjoy our home-grown foods, to celebrate the natural treasures available to us and to live our lives a little closer to the earth.

Flowers in the Fall at Mahone Bay NS where the moderating effect of the ocean gives gardeners a zone 6b.

Daffodils at Cordova Bay, Vancouver Island BC, zone 9.

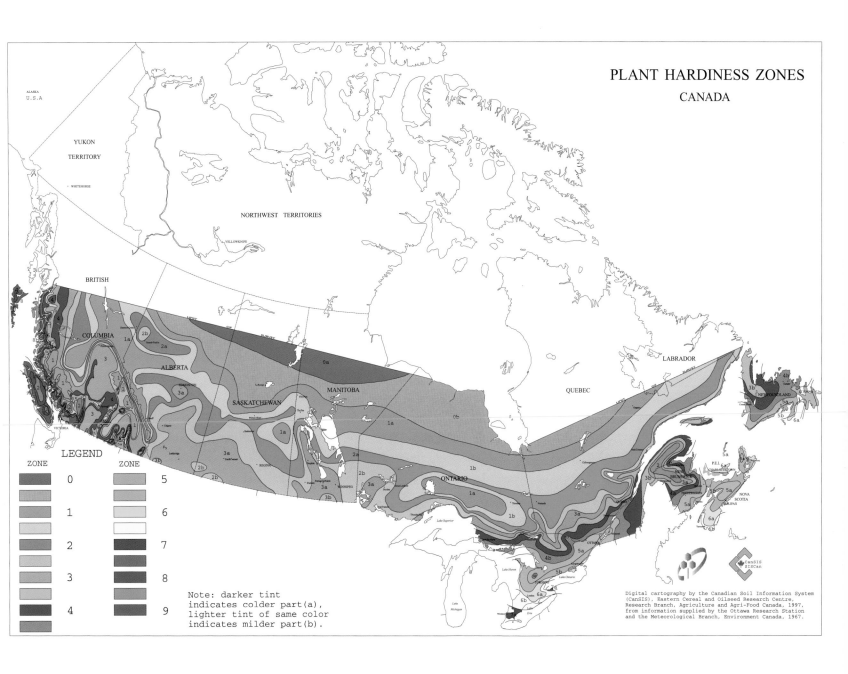

PLANT HARDINESS ZONES
CANADA

LEGEND

ZONE		ZONE	
	0		5
	1		6
	2		7
	3		8
	4		9

Note: darker tint
indicates colder part(a),
lighter tint of same color
indicates milder part(b).

Digital cartography by the Canadian Soil Information System
(CanSIS), Eastern Cereal and Oilseed Research Centre,
Research Branch, Agriculture and Agri-Food Canada, 1997,
from information supplied by the Ottawa Research Station
and the Meteorological Branch, Environment Canada, 1967.

11

The berries of mountain ash are a favourite food for winter birds.

CHAPTER 1

JANUARY

CIRCLE OF THE YEAR

Something gathers up the fragments, and nothing is lost.
Fourcois [1]

A garden is a long-term event so it is not unreasonable to begin in January (or any other month of the year). What we do now can affect next year's garden and the one you have the year after that. What we are aiming for is rich and powerful soil which will grow a luxuriant abundance of foodstuff, most of which we will eat. But some will go back to nourish Mother Earth who will reward us with even more abundance the next year.

It is snowing outside and the garden seems a million miles away. But we do have a bunch of carrots which were grown in somebody's garden. We can cut off the tops and put them in a compost container, add the peelings, too, and the last of the cabbage that doesn't look so good in the crisper. We have already made a direct connection to next summer's garden. We have touched the circle of the year.

Composting is the part of gardening which I find the most exciting. If a gardener is playing God, creating a little world of one's own, then the compost pile is the cradle of creation.

A compost system can be very simple. Mine starts with a deep bowl that sits on the refrigerator. I reason that it is high enough that its contents are not visible (unless you are very tall) and the heat from the refrigerator removes excess moisture. I don't cover it and there's no smell. It does get full often so I empty it almost every day into a black plastic composter which sits outside the back garage door in wintertime. In summertime I move the black bin down to the garden and sometimes use an intermediate pail in the garage to save trips outside.

Composting is a wonderfully natural system that builds upon itself. The trouble is most of us are starting from scratch. We may remember a farm which was a vital hive of growing power where animals produced abundant manure and an underground treasure of established roots sent up rhubarb and asparagus and supported currants and raspberries each year, while an orchard filled the cellar with apples and provided windfalls that went to the pigs to be recycled as manure. But we may have a small city plot from which most of the top soil has been removed and the remaining soil might have its natural range of microorganisms (I fondly call them molygrubs) wiped out by an assortment of chemicals. We might have less to work with than our pioneer ancestors trying to scratch a living between blackened stumps.

Nevertheless let us begin, knowing that our earth can only get better if we add compost. In composting we are accelerating a natural process which would occur anyway if we just threw lettuce or carrot tops out the door. They would go back to nature, release their nutrients to Mother Earth. The trouble is it would take a long time. In composting we are putting a lot of refuse material in one place and using a little knowledge to make it decompose really fast. We end up with a beautiful black magic called humus.

Humus is preferable to commercial fertilizer because it actually improves the soil while it feeds the plant. Commercial fertilizer only feeds the plant. When it is used up, the plant is left a sitting duck in poor, compacted soil, unable to hold moisture. Humus, with its spongy porous composition actually aerates the soil and increases its water-holding capacity. Humus also holds on to nutrients for slow release during the growing season so there is no quick spurt of growth followed by sudden decline.

A compost bin should be at least three feet square by three feet high. It can be the familiar black plastic commercial unit or a garbage can with holes poked in it or a drum with holes. It can be built of wood or cement blocks or made of wire and rods. The problem with units which have access from the top is that you break your back trying to turn the material in order to aerate it. My personal solution to this is to use the black plastic container for holding fresh scraps but keep an active, well-turned pile of compost in a heap beside it. On a small city lot such composting behaviour might be considered messy. An alternative is a four-sided unit with one side hinged to swing open and allow easy access for a fork or spade. It should be made of untreated wood using cedar for the four posts and any untreated scrap wood for the side boards. Or use hardware cloth for the sides, anchoring it to the posts with wire staples. Even more elegant is a three-section bin where you put fresh leaves and weeds and grass and household scraps on the left and move the mixture to the centre as it starts to decompose, then to the right side as it finishes.

Our composter in its winter position

Right now, in January, my kitchen scraps just sit there in the plastic composter outside the garage door, a potato still looking like a potato. But come spring, decomposition will begin. At this point I will move bin and contents (lift the bin off and fork the contents into a wheelbarrow) down to its summer location beside the garden.

Whether you use a bin or an open heap, start with a layer of loose twigs on the bottom to help air to circulate. The recipe for making compost is simply a mix of brown and green; brown materials supplying carbon and green materials supplying nitrogen. Leaves can be used for brown but they should be shredded; otherwise they mat and are not good mixers. Straw, dried grass or corn stalks are brown additions. Grass clippings are excellent greens and are readily available to most homeowners. Add kitchen scraps, weeds. A layer of food scraps can be covered with a thin layer of soil or manure for a ready supply of microorganisms. Layers should be about four inches thick and if dry, should be watered to the wetness of a squeezed out mop or sponge.

An excellent time to make a fast-acting compost pile is May or June when you have abundant materials and abundant heat from the sun. I prefer to do this as an open heap on the ground beside my black composter. Last year's leaves, shredded by running a lawn mower through the pile, are waiting in garbage bags behind the shed to provide the brown layer. Frozen solid now, they'll tumble out crisp and sweet in May. If you have no leaves use straw, dead grasses, sawdust. Green for nitrogen is not hard to find as weeds grow rampant in May and June. Kitchen scraps saved over winter also release nitrogen. Consider chopping them into pieces as small as one inch to help microorganisms break down the material faster. Spring lawns are exuberant with green growing power. Thick heaps of green nitrogen-rich clippings can be raked up for compost, providing the wonderful quick heat that cooks your compost to perfection.

Don't collect clippings from lawns that might have been sprayed with unknown chemicals. I once found an enormous heap of green grass clippings dumped beside a country road. Delighted, I filled ten garbage bags and hauled my treasure home. My compost heated incredibly fast but I began to worry about where that grass had been and what had been used on it. I labelled my compost heap suspicious and used it on flower gardens, not on vegetable plots.

A compost pile three to five feet high and three to five feet wide should heat up to 55°C (130°F) in about three days. Poke your fist into the pile to feel this heat. After three days use a fork to mix the pile. The easiest way to mix it is to actually move it into a new pile beside the old, mixing well as you fork it over. Three

"Can I see what's in there through this crack?"

days later move it back. Keep doing this for two weeks when your compost should be ready for use.

While your special pile was getting this attention you have also been throwing kitchen scraps and garden weeds into the black bin so there is a lot of material to start a new pile along with more leaves and more grass clippings. If you don't want to be actively turning now that it's almost summer, you can build a slow-cooker pile and just leave it alone. The recipe stays the same, the time on the stove is longer.

A compost heap has a few basic needs. One of these is oxygen. Turning loosens the pile and lets air in. Other methods include poking, stirring, lifting and loosening with a fork or putting a perforated pipe into the centre of the heap. There's a special tool for composting which looks like a cane with two small steel wings on the bottom which fold up when you are poking it into the heap, then open up to stir the heap as you lift it up and out. Lack of air in compost results in a heap that smells and may make unhappy neighbours. Compost is like baking bread or pastry, you pay attention to the smell, the texture, the appearance and you develop an extra sense to tell you what is right. For a slow-cooking compost, turning once a week may be enough.

Compost that is too wet or too dry will not work well. Anyone who has rolled out pastry will know the concept of adding a little flour to the board. For compost, use sawdust or dry leaves or straw. If it is too dry the answer of course is water; the trick is to get it into the centre. When building a pile you can gently water each layer. Later on you can poke holes and pour water into the holes. In very dry times shape the top of your heap like a dish to hold water. In early spring keep your heap cone-shaped so the heavy rains will run off.

If rain persists for days you might want to use a plastic cover.

If well-rotted manure is available when you are building a compost pile, a layer on the bottom is an excellent way to provide the microorganisms which will boost action in the heap. Red wigglers found in manure or leaf mould are highly desirable for your compost heap.

There are creatures you don't want in your compost; these include skunks, raccoons, rats and mice. To avoid attracting them never add meat or fish or cooked vegetables which have been buttered or oiled. Always cover kitchen scraps with a layer of soil or grass or weeds. If there is already a problem in your neighbourhood, look at some of the animal-proof containers which are now on the market. If you do find a mouse or a garter snake in your compost it isn't the end of the world. It's more like a compliment. It means you have created a lively ecosystem where wild creatures feel at home.

As the January snow blows outside, the idea of standing out in the garden playing with your compost heap while the sun sits warm on your shoulder and birds sing and you can almost hear the beans and radish grow, sounds too good to be true. But there will be June days when there is too much to do and some of this will feel a lot like work. At such times you will lean on your hoe and wipe the sweat from your face with a dirty hand and ask why. Why am I doing this?

There are some good reasons. A home garden keeps us eating well all year. It puts us in control of what we eat so we know where it was grown, in what soil and who handled it. It lets us feed our families without adding pesticides to their diet.

Diary, Jan. 15: I pull my little granddaughter in a sleigh over the place where the garden is/was. If I tell her about what grows here, will she believe it? Even an adult in January - even myself - can hardly comprehend that a jungle of greenery riots here in summer, crowds together, tangles, tumbles, climbs up on poles, reaches out into the field. Here where there's only white snow. Where there will be only brown ground when the snow melts. Who would believe? What an act of faith a garden is!

Although it is work to dig that soil, pull those weeds and water plants on the hot dry days, it is also a joy to go out at dinner time and harvest the spinach or beans or berries to be eaten within the hour. And we have not had to cart them home from the supermarket, unpack, refrigerate and deal with the styrofoam and plastic garbage they carried on their backs. Even in winter when we harvest our garden vegetables from the freezer, the container is reusable, the vegetable or fruit was not carted north for 1000 miles and three days while the truck added carbon dioxide to the air of America.

Growing a garden provides a real saving in money. When a mother or father loses a job they gain the time to garden on a large scale just when they need it most. They also gain something in spirit, an antidote to the feeling of being laid off, useless, unneeded. In our society we are too liable to equate self-worth with having a job, measuring our worth by the rewards others give us. Real self-worth involves creativity, making something out of nothing, providing for our families ourselves. Every farmer knows this. Almost

every child and young adult raised in the city does not know it. Gardening exemplifies the idea of creativity and production which can make a person grounded and self-secure for a lifetime. Educators are only now beginning to use gardening in city schools to teach these ideals, often with astounding results.

In the rural Ontario community where I grew up many people were poor farmers on sandy, unproductive soil. In the upbeat "progressive" mood of the 1950s when people began taking factory jobs, those who remained on the farms were sometimes considered "backward". From the perspective of the 1990s they look rather good. They had little money for worldly goods but their children went to the one-room schools with lunch boxes well-filled from good gardens in summer and well-stocked larders in winter.

The poor in Canadian cities are only one or two generations removed from those farms. They can re-learn the skills. Immigrants from third-world countries often bring with them a knowledge of growing food and make good use of back yard gardens. A small piece

In the grip of winter.

of city earth, properly tended, can produce a big yield of nutritious edibles.

A stay-at-home mother or father is in danger of feeling alone, cut off from a community of workers at office or factory. Gardening can unite him or her to the neighbourhood and to fellow gardeners. A garden is a conversation piece, a common ground, a shared campaign. (If nothing else, you are fellow warriors in the battle against bugs.)

Planting and weeding and harvesting is also good exercise, cheaper than golf or an exercise club. For the newly retired a garden offers endless possibilities to design or build or conduct scientific experiments while keeping physically, mentally and psychologically fit.

Another advantage of gardening is aligning oneself with the rhythm of the seasons. Primitive people lived according to this rhythm. It could still be extremely important to our well-being but we are often far removed from its cadence. Gardening restores this meaningful tune which resonates so differently in June than in October. Do we want to eat pumpkin pie in June or strawberry shortcake in October? There is immediate discord in the idea. Conversely there is some sense of harmony and well-being in picking snow-peas in spring and harvesting squash when the air is orange with autumn. Each season makes its own demands and offers its own delights. If we move and work according to the circle of the seasons we stay in touch with a mysterious force which contributes in some way to our health and potential for happiness.

Squash stored since October are still good in January. Squash are high in vitamin A and also supply potassium.

SQUASH PUFF

3 cups cooked squash, mashed
½ cup onion, chopped
I tbsp. butter
2 large eggs, separated
¼ cup milk
3 tbsp. flour
3 tsp. baking powder
¾ tsp. salt
⅛ tsp. pepper
½ cup buttered crumbs

Bake squash, then mash. Sauté onion until limp. Beat in egg yolks and milk. Stir in flour, baking powder, salt, pepper. Beat egg whites until stiff. Fold into mixture. Put into casserole and top with buttered crumbs. Bake 25 minutes at 180°C (350°F).

COLESLAW FOR SUBS

I cabbage
I carrot
I onion
I green pepper
Bring to a boil:
⅔ cups white sugar
I cup white vinegar
⅔ cup salad oil
2 tsp. salt
I tsp. each celery seed, mustard seed
½ tsp. turmeric

Chop cabbage, carrot, onion and pepper or use food processor. Pour hot syrup over vegetables. Stir. Cool. Store in glass jars in refrigerator. Keeps one month.

Cabbage belongs to the cruciferous family of vegetables being studied because they contain chemicals believed to have cancer-blocking properties. Cabbage also contains calcium and vitamins E, C and U (helpful for ulcers and other stomach ailments).

RED CABBAGE CASSEROLE

4 to 6 slices bacon
I to 2 onions, sliced
I to 2 apples, chopped
I small to medium cabbage, shredded
¼ cup brown sugar
¼ cup vinegar
I tbsp. ground cloves
¼ cup red wine
salt and pepper

Cook bacon and break into pieces. Put other ingredients in frying pan with one tablespoon bacon fat (or replace with cooking oil). Stir well. Cook on low heat for 30 minutes or put in covered casserole and put in oven for 30 minutes at 180°C (350°F).

Cabbage, carrots and onions are all vegetables you may have stored from your garden. The pepper for your coleslaw will have to come from the supermarket.

The commonest climber for a log house is the hop, which is, as you will find, an indispensable plant in a Canadian garden, it being the principal ingredient in making the yeast with which the household bread is raised. Planted near the pillars of your verandah, it forms a graceful drapery of leaves and flowers, which are pleasing to look upon, and valuable either for use or sale.
Catharine Parr Traill, 1885[1]

Hops at Hillview Organic Farm.

CHAPTER 2

FEBRUARY

THE GARDEN CONNECTION

But will spring ever come ? ...green leaves and flowers, and streams that murmur as they flow, soft summer airs ... can such things be, or do they exist only in poetry and Paradise?

Anna Jameson [2]

A non-gardening friend thinks our garden group is odd because we don't meet in July and August. Gardeners don't have time for meetings in the summer - we are out in the garden picking peas or bachelor's buttons. The time when all of us need the buoyant support of a garden group is February.

Seed catalogues arrive in the Christmas mail to be savoured in the quiet days that start the new year. Gardening magazines are devoured from cover to cover in February. Gardening books, full of how-to ideas, fill a whole section of most public libraries. But best of all is the information and enthusiasm picked up directly from friends and neighbours.

There is a long tradition of sharing associated with gardening. For the early pioneer woman isolated in the bush or on the empty prairie, sharing seeds, produce and recipes with other pioneer women was a lifeline that sometimes saved her from loneliness and despair while it helped to feed her family. Catharine Parr Traill lived at Lakefield, Ontario in the 1830s near where I

live now in the 1990s. When she writes, "I am anxiously looking forward to the spring, that I may get a garden laid out in front of the house; as I mean to cultivate some of the native fruits and flowers, which, I am sure, will improve greatly by culture,"[3] I feel a bond with her across a century and a half. I can picture her getting together with her sister, Susanna Moodie, on a snowy winter evening to trade seeds of pumpkin and corn and discuss how they will plant them in spring.

For the gently-reared English lady the study of plants was an ardent affair which made her life in the backwoods of Canada not a hardship to be endured but an exploration to be pursued with delight. Writing to a botanist friend in England she says, "How often do I wish you were beside me in my rambles among the woods and clearings: you would be so delighted in searching out the floral treasures of the place."[4]

Each of us when we embark on gardening enters a new country where we have not wandered before, where there are hundreds of vegetables and flowers and

Log cabin and garden at Lang Century Village.

"Even Johnnie's little garden flourished, although his methods were not always the best. One day his mother found him pulling up beans and dipping their heads into a pail of water to give them a drink." [5]

As they struggled to feed a large family on a bush farm, Anna could supplement the small income David got from logging or mining, with the sale of vegetables to a logging camp.

In a letter home she describes one year's garden: "Then comes a broad strip of peas for the pig, then a large sowing of garden peas for ourselves. If we cannot sell them green, they will make splendid pea soup in the winter. Then I have a large piece of beans for use both green and dried, as well as several long rows of broad beans. Then comes a large bed of onions, half belongs to the boys. We can make 4 shillings or a dollar a bushel of them. Then I have beds of parsnips, carrots, radishes, and lettuces, and my strawberries are in blossom." [6]

Anna and Catharine had no garden magazines, few books and no public libraries. Letters to and from family members and gardening friends in England provided a tenuous line of support.

Anna writes: "How glad I was to get a letter from you at last. I thought you never were going to write again ... .

"Give my love to dear Father. I was glad to see his handwriting again, even if it was only the address on the envelope. We are having hot weather now. People are prophesying a hot summer; it seems like it. Everything is fresh and green in the woods. I wish you could see it all." [7]

Catharine writes: "Our woods and clearings are now full of beautiful flowers. You will be able to form some idea of them from the dried specimens that I send you.

fruits and grasses and weeds, not to mention bugs and butterflies and bees and insects, all important to us if we can get to know them.

Anna Leveridge pioneered in the 1880s. Her bush farm near Bancroft was more isolated in the 1880s than Catharine's had been in the 1830s. Her letters home to England express the joy of gardening with her children. After the trees were cut they began to create a forest garden where nature had laid down humus century after century forming a rich soil layer on the Precambrian rock of the Canadian Shield.

"Soon the whole family was intensely proud of the results. Fed by the richness of the new soil and watered by frequent spring showers, the garden grew splendidly. When there had been no rain for a week or more, the children carried pails of water from a creek flowing by near the edge of the garden. Like other things that are loved and get the attention they crave, everything Anna and her children planted thrived luxuriantly through the first few years in the new home.

You will recognize among them many of the cherished pets of our gardens and greenhouses, which are here flung carelessly from Nature's lavish hand among our woods and wilds." [8]

In another letter she says, "The first time you send a parcel or box, do not forget to enclose flower-seeds, and the stones of plums, damsons, bullace, pips of the best kinds of apples ... ." [9]

Catharine was fortunate enough to have a friend in Peterborough named Frances Stewart who had brought with her a copy of Frederick Pursh's *North American Flora* describing 700 species of American plant life. "This work was lent to me by a friend, the only person I knew who had paid any attention to botany as a study, and to whom I was deeply indebted for many hints and for the cheering interest that she always took in my writings. ... My next teachers were old settlers' wives, and choppers and Indians. These gave me knowledge of another kind, and so by slow steps, I gleaned my plant lore... ." [10]

Today a person interested in gardening in Canada has no shortage of companionship. Groups exist in every city where ideas can be exchanged and lifelong friendships established. Looking back at topics my garden group has shared in monthly get-togethers, I find that we have learned about herbs, discussed edible weeds, cooked up new and rare (to us) vegetables, studied seed-starting in spring, made herb wreaths in fall, learned about perennials and some of the history of flowers, planted window boxes, learned lawn care and visited special gardens in our area.

In several cities demonstration organic gardens have been established to promote ecological education, community cooperation and food production for poverty relief and ecological education. In 1981

Cathy Dueck at Peterborough's Ecology Park. Founder and director of the park, she has worked for 25 years in ecological horticulture. She is a dynamic force in natural restoration of shoreline and woodland, in the greening of school yards and the planning and promoting of community gardens and parks.

23

Garden group at
Peterborough
Ecology Park

Michael Levenston, a pioneer in this movement, founded such a garden in Vancouver. Now in the 1990s there are ecological gardens in cities across Canada, some established by municipalities seeking a green alternative to herbicide-dependent parks, some established by chapters of Canadian Organic Growers or by garden groups. Being part of such an initiative provides excitement and learning that goes beyond the simple goal of taking vegetables home for dinner.

Peterborough's Ecology Garden was established in 1991 on a 25 by 100-foot plot loaned by the city for an educational garden. Here an enthusiastic group of organic gardeners began to demonstrate urban greening and a return to harmony between nature and humankind.

By 1994 the garden, under the direction of Cathy Dueck, had lushly outgrown its plot and was moved to a larger site where a small creek flows into Little Lake beside Beavermead Park. It is a wonderful place to visit, to attend workshops on Sunday afternoons, a place where you can learn about edible landscaping or good bugs/bad bugs, or ground covers or seed-saving or no-till gardening; discuss your problems with experienced gardeners and share your ideas.

During spring and fall school groups visit to learn about food production and garden skills and sustainable lifestyle. Visits are connected to subjects the classroom group is studying ... insects, trees, harvest, waste reduction. During summertime children, aged six to ten, can attend "Earth Adventures" programs where scavenger hunts, garden activities, crafts and storytelling are used to explore themes like "Beautiful Bugs" or "The Magic Forest" or "The Secret Garden".

A garden is a place where a child can study birds and insects and butterflies first hand.

Many cities now have community gardens which turn otherwise vacant land into flourishing gardens and inviting green space where families can work and play. Peterborough has 14 community gardens, nine of them started by the YWCA. The Y's Garden Coordinator Joan Mercer works to find suitable garden plots and to match would-be gardeners , usually low-income families, with a nearby garden. Gardens are located on city property, on the grounds of Sir Sandford Fleming College, at housing complexes. One garden was started by Trent University students who invited the public to join them. A plot behind Northminster United Church costs $5 and is available to anyone needing green space.

Joan Mercer says , "The need for fresh affordable food is often what motivates people. But also important is the chance to meet other people, to dig in the dirt, to relax out-of-doors and to be amazed at what you grow."

Since 1975 the city of Montreal has had a large scale community project which lets 10,000 people use 6,700 garden plots, each about 200 feet square. In all of these gardens the use of chemicals is forbidden.

If you must plant something in February and you can't find the chives under the snow, grab a sprouted

Years ago when I was still gardening with chemical fertilizers, an enthusiastic voice on CBC radio was telling of another way to garden. Mary Perlmutter was a pioneer in Canadian organic gardening and an organizer of Canadian Organic Growers. She has talked to hundreds of garden groups and shared her ideas through the media. Now gardeners have joined her en masse. Here she shows her garden at Blythe School near Fenelon Falls to a group of gardeners from Peterborough.

onion from your own supply or buy it at the supermarket, put it into a pot and watch for the tall green shoots to add to your stir frys and potato dishes. Take slips from that leggy geranium you've been nursing along and get them ready for spring. Start pots of herbs like basil or parsley or chives which need time to get growing. If they do well you can start using them from the pots before you plant them in the garden. Another thing you can do is to make jam from the strawberries and raspberries and currants and rhubarb you froze last summer when you were so busy. But don't plant seeds for garden vegetables; it's too soon.

Diary, Feb. 10: I just went out to the garden, shovel in hand, to see if I could pry out a root of chives. I couldn't even find them. It is obvious that I'm getting gardener's itchy-thumb two months too soon. This is where friends and fellow gardeners come in. When you can't dig and plant you can talk and plan.

Catharine Parr Traill's Johnny Cake:
"Take a quart of sour milk or buttermilk,
to which add as much soda or pearl-ash
as will make it froth up well; thicken
this milk with Indian-meal; add a little
salt; pour the batter into a flat pan, and
bake it brown; cut in pieces, and eat it
hot with butter or molasses."

When stretched entirely over broccoli,
row covers keep pests out.

Cauliflower is a cruciferous vegetable believed to contain cancer-fighting substances. It is high in fibre, vitamin C and potassium, also contains calcium and iron.

Broccoli is probably the most potent of the cruciferous vegetables. Research suggests that it protects against stomach, colon and lung cancers. It also supplies abundant vitamin A.

CAULIFLOWER FLOWER
1 cauliflower (whole)
½ cup salad dressing
½ cup grated parmesan cheese
½ cup bread crumbs

Microwave cauliflower in ½ in. water for 5 minutes. Place in greased baking dish. Mix salad dressing and parmesan cheese. Spread over cauliflower, then sprinkle bread crumbs over cheese. Bake at 180°C (350°F) for 10-15 minutes.

QUICK BROCCOLI CASSEROLE
1 head fresh broccoli
1 can cream of celery soup
²/₃ cup shredded cheddar cheese
2 slices whole wheat bread in crumbs
2 tbsp. melted butter

Cook broccoli 5 minutes. Chop into 2 in. pieces and put in casserole. Top with soup, then cheese. Melt butter in frying pan. Stir bread crumbs into the butter, then put on top of casserole. 180°C (350°F) for 30 minutes.

Heavy horses have become popular on some farms again to plant crops or pull sleighs.

CHAPTER 3

MARCH
GROUNDED

Global sustainability begins with the discovery that there is no battlefield in the back yard.

Cathy Dueck [1]

Grounded is a term used by those who practice yoga. It means having your two feet firmly planted on the ground and feeling the connection of that stability through strong well-stretched legs allowing flexibility in the back that will enable you both to bend and to stand up straight. Being grounded allows not only physical movement, it releases the mind to move freely with the body. This seems to me a wonderful image for gardening. I picture the "grounded" person planting onions or picking beans, his or her legs a powerful base which lets the torso move to left or right and, best of all, lets the gardener straighten up afterward.

This doesn't always happen (the straightening up), particularly if the gardener is over 50. A gardener can prevent a lot of stiffness and possible grief by preceding the intense outdoor work of May and June with a stretch-and strengthening exercise class. Winter provides a piece of available time for this. Yoga or Tai-Chi or any of the low-impact aerobic classes can make a difference in how easy it is to hoe that row and lift that pail when real gardening begins.

Looking at it the other way around, gardening is the perfect complement to an exercise program. It helps you to keep fit from April to October, all in your own back yard. I just spoke to a 98-year-old friend who had been ill. She told me it was nothing but an attack of old age and she had rallied from it nicely. I remember the garden she had around her small house on Lake Katchewanooka and I wonder how much it helped her stave off those 'attacks of old age' until her late nineties.

When she was still in her home in her early nineties she made a decision to let her garden go wild. When weeding became too difficult she simply enjoyed it in another way, letting the perennials survive if they could and share space with wild weeds and flowers of the field. There was no battlefield in her back yard.

29

Keeping a connection with the earth becomes increasingly difficult in our society. Driving past the massive housing projects on the outskirts of Toronto, we notice that there are no children playing in the rare field or creek valley that remains. Are parents afraid to let their children out to play or are the fields so unattractive, so denuded of the natural that kids prefer the malls?

Most children have a genuine curiosity and ease with the natural world which our housing development-car-mall mentality is destroying. A few schools are finding ways to re-find the wonderment. At a school in Toronto violence had become so rampant that parents were pulling their children out of the school. One mother refused to do this. Instead, she mobilized her neighbours to break up the concrete which covered the school's yard (originally an orchard) and plant a garden. The terraced garden which the children helped to build and plant and then to tend and protect, became a place where small bodies and minds could be truly grounded, where they could see butterflies and bugs and flowers opening in the sun; where they could harvest and eat vegetables they themselves planted. Suddenly there was a waiting list to get children into this school.

In many Canadian cities a green-up initiative is working to make school yards natural, productive, useful and inspiring to the children who play there. Henry Kock, horticulturalist of the Arboretum at University of Guelph, remembers standing on concrete in his school yard with his face pressed against a chain link fence looking out to the woods which were fenced out of the students' lives. That particular forest is gone now so a child couldn't even look out to the green places. But some of the wildness is moving back where it belongs, inside the fence, with the kids.

Gardeners come in all sizes.

Three family members against the weeds.

A reporter with *The Peterborough Examiner* calls it "a small ecological revolution going on in urban elementary school playgrounds". The wilderness gardens at Peterborough schools have lured in rabbits, chipmunks, toads, butterflies, praying mantis, a variety of birds. Children learn that a single toad can eat 10,000 garden bugs as an alternative to chemical spray.

The concept of working with nature is being learned by the children who volunteer at noon-hour to plant and water and harvest. The diversity of nature is understood by kids who see high-bush cranberry, milkweed, a jack-in-the-pulpit. Children learn that a garden is more than a cropped green lawn - it is native shrubs, ground covers, swamp grasses, trees and vines, shady places, wild foods as well as foods you grow from seed, wild flowers as well as flowers you plant from nursery six-packs. They learn to compost, putting green left-overs from their lunches and green garden weeds together with brown leaves and straw to make new soil. Best of all, they take their hands-on new-discovery ideas home. Children are teaching their parents.

Because of our industrialized life, our division of labour, our jobs which produce mostly paper, our removal from the earth to the skyscraper, from the farm to the factory, the 'productive' middle years of our lives may be the least productive in terms of contentment, awareness, sensitivity to our environment, well-being and togetherness of body, mind and spirit. It may be left to our children and to our grandpas and grandmas to keep us grounded in a reality which is earth-bound.

In a little book called *Root People* which I discovered in a school library, the children of nature are all asleep below the ground as spring approaches. They wake up, comb their hair, get dressed, and then, led by Mother Nature, they march out carrying grasses, flowers, butterflies, ladybugs. They play all summer in the fields and woods and when they begin to shiver in the fall, they march back underground again. For small children, it catches the magic that is nature, the wonder of the garden of the wild.

While we wait in March for the outdoor root people to wake up, many indoor gardeners are busy starting seed. What is needed for this operation is a lot of faith. Faith against damping-off in particular. Faith in yourself to keep the moisture right and not to leave the tomatoes too long in hot sun on the patio on day one of hardening off.

Two bits of knowledge are needed before you begin planting:

1. The probable date of the last frost in your area.

2. The number of weeks a particular plant needs to reach transplant size from seed.

Starting too early can cause problems as your plants outgrow their accommodation becoming tall and gangly, tempting you to set them out too soon. Experienced gardeners have seen how the smaller transplant adapts more easily to the move outdoors and quickly catches up in size to the big one started a month earlier.

Soil for starting seeds must be sterile. If you use your own soil, bake it at 82°C (180°F) for 30 to 45 minutes.

Mix it with equal portions of peat moss and sand or peat moss and perlite. An easier way is to buy a bag of soilless mix at a garden store.

Containers can be wood or plastic flats or individual peat boxes available at garden stores or plastic six-packs from last year's bedding plants. Or a milk carton laid on its side with the top cut off.

After the seeds are sown, cover with plastic to keep in moisture but leave a small opening to allow some circulation. Keep warm by placing near a register or on top of the refrigerator. For most seeds, light is not needed until the seeds germinate.

Once they do and the covering is removed, plants want all the light they can get. Many gardeners supplement sunlight with a fluorescent grow-light. Ideally the seedlings would like 12 to 15 hours of light a day, more than they can get in a south-facing window in March and April. One way to increase light units is to hang aluminum foil behind the plant shelf to reflect the sunlight back to the plants and double their exposure. I also line the shelf or windowsill with foil to reflect more light up to the plants.

Label plants by writing on popsicle sticks or a strip of plastic cut from a margarine or yoghurt container. Insert these into the soil.

To thin seedlings simply cut off the weaker ones with scissors right at soil level leaving roots in the soil.

Transplanting to richer soil should occur as soon as the first true leaves appear. Lift by the leaves, not the stem. Bury in soil up to the leaves. Water carefully, then let plants rest without water or direct sunlight for a day or two until they look well again. Move back to the light and begin fertilizing with fish emulsion each week.

Let a lettuce plant go to seed in your herb garden and you'll find a patch of lettuce already planted next April.

Damping-off is the bogey man of seed starting. The non-organic solution is a chemical fungicide. Using this on vegetables you will later eat seems questionable at best. An organic approach is to use garlic-flavoured water. A preventative approach is to keep the planting medium moist but not soaking wet.

Hardening-off is the process of adjusting plants to the real world. Cut down on watering, stop fertilizing and place the flats outside for an hour or two a day, not in direct sunlight at first.

Favourite plants for starting indoors are tomatoes and peppers and squash and cantaloupe, plants that need a head start in a warm environment.

Meanwhile in the kitchen department is there anything left to eat which is remotely connected to the garden? Oh yes there is. Parsnips store themselves in the ground covered with eight to ten inches of leaves or straw in our zone 5 location. Then, in early spring when home-grown vegetables are as rare as hen's teeth, you dig up beautiful white, very sweet parsnips.

My garden diary notes March 28 one year, April 3 another year as parsnip digging days. This will vary according to zone and the late or early arrival of spring weather. A certain smell in the air, or maybe the sound of red-winged blackbirds, will tell you when it is time to dig the parsnips. Don't wait until they sprout.

Diary: March 28: Digging parsnips is not a chore. It is a first ritual of spring. The temperature is 13°C (55°F) and the air is very still without the cruel wind that brought snow yesterday. Some of the long white roots lift out easily, others break off because deep down the earth is still hard with frost. I put the roots in a pail of water and scrub them with a plastic pot scrubber, amazed at how easily they become clean and white. There are birds singing and a gentle laid-back hum is in the air. It's like a final early-morning snooze before the earth wakes up and all the little root people get moving again.

Carrots left growing under 20 inches of loose leaves can be dug any time during the winter. But let's hope we put a flag stick at either end so it will be possible to find them under the snow.

Parsnips supply abundant potassium and are high in fibre.

BAKED PARSNIPS
1 egg
6 parsnips cut in strips
onion-garlic bread crumbs
1 cube of pesto (recipe on p. 88)
Fluff egg with a fork. Dip parsnip strips into the egg, then into the bread crumbs. Place strips on a cookie sheet. Let pesto cube melt on a saucer then dribble its oil and herbs over the parsnips. Bake at 180°C (350°F) about 1 hour.

Carrots are high in beta-carotene, vitamin B-complex, C, D, E and K, iron, calcium, phosphorous, sodium, potassium, magnesium, manganese, sulphur and copper. Carrots, particularly raw carrots, are a powerful food.

CARROT CASSEROLE
6 to 8 carrots, grated
2 to 3 tbsp. butter
1 tbsp. chopped mint
salt and pepper
1 tsp. sugar
Layer grated carrots in greased casserole dotting each layer with butter and sprinkling with salt, pepper and sugar. Do this three times. Bake at 180°C (350°F) for 45 minutes.

GLAZED PARSNIPS AND CARROTS
If you left a row of carrots in the garden (covered with leaves or straw) you should have fresh carrots for this excellent combination. Parsnip-digging time is maple syrup time so use this seasonal wonder for your glaze.

3 or 4 parsnips
3 or 4 carrots
2 tbsp. butter
2 tbsp. maple syrup or brown sugar
2 tbsp. orange juice
Slice parsnips and carrots lengthwise. Cook in water about five minutes. Drain. Add butter, maple syrup and orange juice and cook and stir until the juice becomes a glaze on the parsnips and carrots.

Parsnips

On the land again.

CHAPTER 4

APRIL
GETTING DOWN TO EARTH

Those who labor in the earth are the chosen people of God.
Thomas Jefferson [1]

Farmers have a phrase -"getting on the land". It conjures up images of anxious, eager waiting, of watching the rain come down, tramping out to the field in rubber boots and lifting a handful of soil to feel if it's ready yet. A farmer knows his soil inside out; he knows if it is heavy clay or light sand or the best of loam; he knows what manure he put on it when, what crop he grew in it last year, what he wants in it this year. He knows how long it took to dry out last year, how good or bad last year's crop was, how he hopes to improve it this time around.

The more a gardener knows his/her soil the better a garden will grow. If in doubt about what you have, soil can be tested at government agricultural offices. Loam is dark and crumbly, full of organic material, an evenly balanced combination of sand, silt and clay. It handles water well. All it needs is organic matter for the perfect growing medium. Most of us have too much of either sand or clay. Sand warms up quickly in the spring but

lets water and nutrients pass through too quickly. It can be amended by adding plenty of organic matter - peat moss, leaf mould, compost.

Clay has close packed particles. It is slow to dry out in springtime and stays cold too long. Clay is the land that farmers "can't get on" in the spring. It is land that is hard to work with a garden shovel; when dry it becomes hard like a rock. To amend it large amounts of organic material are needed - compost, manure, leaf mould, peat moss. You can also add sand or sawdust.

Getting to know the pH of your soil is another matter. The pH scale ranges from 0 to 14 with 0 indicating totally acid and 14 indicating totally alkaline. A measure of 7 indicates a neutral soil condition. Most vegetables like to grow in soil that measures between 6 and 6.8.

If you have your soil tested and discover that it is too acidic you can amend it with dolomite (limestone) or with bone meal, wood ashes, or eggshells. Too much

Garden companion.

alkalinity can be counteracted by pine needles, peat moss, or cottonseed meal.

When we dream in January of planting a garden in May, we dream that someone has already spaded up a beautiful plot of earth and we just have to put in the seeds. Fact is nobody has spaded it up if you are a new gardener. In fact there is no garden to spade. There is lawn with rock-hard tenacious roots which you will have to turf out and shake and hassle and swear at.

If you plan far enough ahead there might be an easier way. You can buy black landscape fabric (or black plastic) 3 to 4 feet wide at a garden or hardware store, spread it on the lawn and let those roots turn yellow and die. Put it down in September or October if possible; if not, be out there the moment the snow goes. Even two months will make a big difference in the work you'll do later.

My garden sits between lawn and hay field and each year the hay field encroaches on the garden and has to be laboriously dug out. I now use black landscape fabric along the hay field edge. This effectively stops the growth of grasses and weeds and makes my sod-turning job much easier in spring.

I also used black landscape fabric to convert an area of lawn to crown vetch. I first dug up three narrow rows about six inches wide in the sod, then spread the fabric (which lets in water but not light), then along the rows I cut short slits in the fabric, put the vetch plants in these holes and left the patch alone for two months except for occasional watering.

By early July the vetch plants were reaching out runners. I removed the black fabric and found good ground with grassroots breaking down to enrich the soil. A small amount of work with a hand spade made the ground ready for all those new runners. By August I had a nice flowering patch of crown vetch covered with pink flowers replacing a piece of lawn we no longer wanted to mow.

Right now in April, we had better get at the digging. This can be done with a shovel or a roto-tiller. A rotary tiller is useful for large garden areas but for the small garden, digging has a lot to recommend it. It uses no fossil fuel. It's thorough because you personally remove every piece of twitch grass and pig weed; the roto-tiller tends to chop up the weeds which will often grow again.

A favourite digging technique is the trench method. Dig eight inches deep and a foot wide along one edge of the garden. Actually lift the soil into a wheel barrow to be put on the far side of the garden. Now dig row number two and put that soil into trench number one,

Crown vetch is a ground cover which will bloom from late spring through summer. Poppies, once established, seed themselves and provide the early summer garden with superb blooms.

adding shovelfuls of compost as you go. For double-digging use a fork to loosen the soil in the bottom of the trench before putting in the new soil. When you have reached the far end of the garden you have the earth in the wheel barrow to put into your final trench along with some compost.

For established gardens some gardeners, me included, do a very shallow digging with a shovel or hoe, the theory being that your nutrients are in the top four inches of earth and you don't want to be turning these down under. Some people also believe that deep digging will bring up dormant weed seeds which will be happy to grow in their new surface location.

Not all gardeners have a piece of land to dig up. At the opposite extreme from the country gardener-cum-farmer is the apartment dweller. People with limited access to the earth can grow vegetables and flowers in window boxes, barrels, tubs, hanging baskets and pots made of clay, wood, plastic and peat.

I discovered growing things in pots when I lived for one year on Vancouver Island in a house by the sea. In September we moved into a small A-frame house with decks on the east and west sides sporting empty planters. To my amazement the stores laid out a vast array of bedding plants in September - winter pansies, heather, chrysanthemums. Coming from zone 5 in Ontario, I was like a kid in a candy store planting my treasures while my friends back home were throwing the frozen vines on the compost heap.

That winter I had to cover my planters and pots two or three times when cold snaps hit the island. The rest of the time they thrived and bloomed and were a real delight. Although I moved back to Ontario, I remain a confirmed pot-gardener.

Containers for flowers and vegetables and herbs can
be anything from flower pots to bathtubs and buggies.

Here, too, I tried pots on both sides of the house but with no Pacific Ocean to modify the heat, my south-facing pots cooked; I soon learned to concentrate on the north side of the house. There I grow mostly flowers - geraniums, petunias, lobelia, alyssum, impatience, godetia - but I also find it convenient to have parsley, chives and other herbs handy outside the door. Peppermint-flavoured mint is nice growing by the back door since I use the leaves to make tea. Since peppers do poorly in my garden I am also growing peppers in a pot by the door, giving them a fertilizer of liquid seaweed to make up for their confined space.

There are some real advantages to container gardening:
  -Almost no need to weed.
  -The possibility of amending soil in one pot for acid-loving plants, in another pot providing soil for those which need a higher pH.
  -The ease of moving a plant when it needs more or less sun.
  -The opportunity to move plants indoors when frost threatens in spring and fall.

Another attraction is the artistic possibilities of different shaped pots, made of different materials, the fun of arranging these on deck or patio or along a walk. For persons confined to a wheel chair or persons of limited mobility, container gardening may be something they can manage.

A few considerations make pot-gardening easier. Light-coloured pots are preferable to black if your patio or balcony is a hot location. Larger pots will be easier to keep watered. Grouping pots together also helps to conserve moisture. Using large peat pots makes it easier to move plants from place to place; clay pots in large sizes are too heavy to move. Any pot will be much heavier if it has just been watered. Remember that lifting a heavy pot from ground level can be very hard on your back. Keep it at a higher level or plan not to move it all summer. A Christmas gift last year will make it easier for me to move potted plants around -a big red wagon.

Water will be needed almost daily for container gardening. A soil moisture probe available from garden stores will help you know when plants need water. Fertilizer will be needed at two-week intervals to keep flowers blooming or vegetables producing at their best.

If you do have some land around your dwelling place you can have rhubarb in early spring. There's probably not a farm house in Canada without a rhubarb patch. No wonder. Easy to grow, ever-lasting and delicious to eat, it is sometimes known as pie-plant. If planting for the first time try to beg, borrow or buy a reddish-stemmed rhubarb for sweet taste. Plant the root in early spring or fall in a trench two feet deep filled to the one foot level with well-rotted manure or compost, with a shovelful of bone meal or rock phosphate and two of granite dust or greensand. Fill in the top 12 inches with top soil. Divide your root into crown pieces with healthy buds and plant the crown one to three inches deep, three feet apart.

When plants have grown about four inches mulch with straw. Wait until the second year to take a few stocks. By the third year harvest half the stocks (never more) from each plant. Pull and twist to remove. Rhubarb leaves are poisonous because of high amounts of oxalates. Lesser amounts occur in the stalk which we eat and may be a problem for some people with a tendency to kidney stones.

Young asparagus plants.

Rhubarb can be cut up and frozen raw or put in a crisp or pie which can then be frozen. If it still looks good in the garden when strawberries ripen in June, the combination of rhubarb and strawberry makes a wonderful jam or pie.

If you are wondering what to do in the garden on that first warm day when the soil is workable, feed your asparagus with a mixture of lime and compost worked into the soil along the row. Asparagus is the green essence of springtime in Canada. Later on its delicate ferns grace the summer garden until they turn golden in autumn when they should be cut down.

An important growing requirement for asparagus is patience. If planted as crowns you will wait until the third season to harvest. If planted as seed your wait will be four or five years. Cut when the stalks are 15 to 20 cm (6 to 8 in.) tall and about the size of your little finger.

When planting asparagus crowns dig a trench 14 inches deep. In the bottom place a one-inch layer of crushed limestone, topped by a three-inch layer of well-rotted manure or compost. Set out the roots 12 inches apart. Cover with four inches of soil; gradually fill in as the asparagus grows.

Diary, April 18: Only an optimist in zone 5 would be putting rhubarb and asparagus in an April chapter. My garden diary for one year notes that rhubarb came through the ground March 28 but cold weather followed and no leaves appeared until April 23. However, in a warm location, in a warmer year, in a warmer climate zone or even in a more sheltered sunny location of your property, rhubarb will be available in April and asparagus soon after.

Rhubarb supplies vitamin C, potassium and lots of fibre.

FAVOURITE RHUBARB PIE
Rhubarb chopped in one in. pieces.
I cup sugar
2 tbsp. flour
pinch of salt
gratings of I lemon
2 eggs
Fill pie shell with rhubarb. Mix other ingredients and pour over rhubarb. Roll out top crust and cut in strips, then arrange on pie lattice fashion. Bake at 205°C (400°F) for 15 minutes, then turn oven to 180°C (350°F) and bake until done.

RHUBARB COFFEE CAKE
I½ cups brown sugar
½ cup margarine or butter
I egg beaten
I tsp. vanilla
2 cups flour
I tsp. salt
I cup sour milk or buttermilk
I tsp. soda (put in milk)
I½ cups rhubarb
Mix all ingredients together and put into a 9x13x3 in. cake pan. Top with a mixture of:
½ cup flour
¼ to ½ cup brown sugar
½ cup butter
½ tsp. cinnamon
Bake at 190°C (375°F) 45-55 minutes.

Asparagus is high in vitamins A, B-complex and C and has potassium, iron and manganese. In springtime it needs very little embellishment. Cook until tender in a steamer which fits into your cooking pot. Or stand the stalks upright in a tall pot and cook in two in. of water. Serve plain or top with lemon juice and melted butter or bread crumbs sauteed in butter with chopped chives and parsley.

ASPARAGUS WITH CREAM CHEESE
2 pounds asparagus cooked
I package (3 oz.) cream cheese
I tbsp. milk
In a teflon fry pan melt and stir cream cheese and milk until blended. Add ½ cup fresh chives. Pour over asparagus and serve.

Digging a garden at
Ground Covers
Unlimited near Bethany,
Ontario.

CHAPTER 5

MAY

DAYS OF SUN AND SALADS

[Salads are] proper for all seasons, but particularly from the beginning of February to July, in which period they are in greatest perfection, and consequently act most effectually in cleansing and attenuating the blood ... .

Alexander Murray [1]

May in Canada is a month brimming with possibility. The possibility of planting a garden. The possibility of not getting it ruined by a late frost. The possibility that it will grow. Hope springs eternal but more so in May.

Tradition in my part of Canada in zone 5, puts the 24th of May as the magic date for frost-free planting. This means that precious tomato and pepper plants started indoors should not be set out until the "long weekend" which falls on the Monday before the 24th. I also pay attention to the moon. If it is full that weekend and temperatures are dipping down I might wait a few more days.

If you live on Lake Ontario you fall into the warmer zone 6. On the shores of Lake Erie you bask in zone 7 or even zone 8 and your magic frost free date moves up by at least two weeks.

Canada's prairie region sits in zone 3 or 4 which means a shorter growing season. High areas of the Rocky Mountains may have to deal with zone 2 conditions. Maritime growers may bask in zone 7 in southern Nova Scotia and along the east shore and even on Newfoundland's Burin Peninsula; or they may have to deal with zone 3 in inland areas of New Brunswick and Quebec .

When I lived on Vancouver Island (zone 9) I was ready to plant vegetables in March beguiled by the camellias, rhododendrons and azaleas in full bloom.

"No, no," I was told, "the ground is much too cold; your seeds will rot, wait until almost the same time as in Ontario to plant your heat-loving crops." Perhaps the best advice is to do as the Romans do; listen to your neighbours, particularly the older ones.

Certain vegetables don't mind having cold toes. Spinach can start life in earth that is close to freezing although it prefers about $16^{\circ}C$ ($60^{\circ}F$). It will germinate best if soaked for a day before planting. As soon as any garden soil can be dug up, plant the seed directly outside. Cold loving varieties can be on the table in six weeks supplying high amounts of vitamins A and B2 as well as iron, calcium and protein.

Four to six weeks before the last frost is the recommended time for planting broccoli, cabbage, lettuce, onions, peas, potatoes, spinach and turnips. In zone 5 or 6 this lets you plant at the end of April.

Beets, carrots, parsnips and radishes can go in two to four weeks before the May 24 magic date in zone 5 (earlier in zones numbered higher). On or about the magic date put in beans, cucumbers, squash, corn.

If the weather remains cold, getting your garden in two weeks before the May long weekend will not make a lot of difference. Gardens grow poorly in cold wet soil. The garden planted later in warm soil may catch

Spring promise.

up to the early one. You can warm the soil considerably by covering it with black polythene (garbage bags split apart work well) for two weeks before planting. What you would like is a soil temperature of 10°C (50°F). Use a soil thermometer (available at garden centres) and take your reading 25 mm (1 in.) deep.

Some gardeners who can't wait like to hedge their bets. They plant half their beets or carrots. Two weeks later if the row hasn't come up or appears very sparse, they replant or fill in, then plant the second half. If Mother Nature was in a fine warm mood, they have two crops nicely spaced two weeks apart.

Lettuce is an undemanding vegetable which can be planted as soon as you can work the ground. It can easily handle night-time temperatures of -10°C (14°F). By using row covers you can help it survive temperatures at and below the freezing mark. It takes very little from the soil so a spring crop can be taken off and the row replanted with beans or beets.

On March 20 I transplanted lettuce seedlings into two 10-inch plastic pots, 14 plants per pot, each little seedling about 2 inches from its neighbour. In such crowded conditions the plants need extra fertilizer, so I gave them seaweed fertilizer twice a week. I set them in the doorway of our south-facing garage, pushing them back and closing the door on very cold nights.

By late April and early May we had lettuce to eat in small amounts. It never did really well possibly because of cool cloudy weather. In fact it looked so poorly in May that I considered throwing it out. Instead I stuck the plants in my herb garden near the garage door. The plants soon took off and far surpassed the lettuce planted directly into the garden. A heat-resistant, black-seeded Simpson type sold by T&T Seeds, this lettuce provided good eating until the mid-July hot spell.

A simple way to provide yourself with early lettuce is to plant it in the fall. Mother Nature will make the decision about when it should sprout in the spring.

The traditional vegetable garden is a rectangle which makes it easy to lay out rows using a string stretched tightly between two sticks and moved to mark each row, spacing the rows according to directions on your seed envelopes. Plant seeds according to package directions but in heavy clay make the planting more shallow and be careful not to bury seeds under hard clumps of soil. The soil covering the seeds should be fine. Some gardeners suggest mixing fine seed like carrots with sand or coffee grounds, then spreading it atop the row to avoid too-deep planting. Water with a fine mist and never allow the ground to dry out until germination is complete.

There is no law requiring a garden to have four sides. As our concept of lawns is changing, our concept of gardens changes too. People are digging up entire front lawns allowing flowers and vegetables to romp together in happy confusion. Herbs are particularly attractive in a flower garden, but curly lettuce, spinach, beans, onions and squash all contribute luxuriant greens and attractive shapes.

Walls and fences invite row gardens. Snow peas can be planted early in April (in zone 5) against a south-facing wall. Rail fences are wonderful for training sweet peas or climbing beans or even cucumbers and squash. A trellis allows beans or squash or cucumbers to grow vertically. Some gardeners fasten a bicycle wheel atop a pole, plant their pole beans beneath it, then run strings from the wheel to the ground and fasten them with stakes.

Seeds started indoors should be ready for transplanting on your frost-free date. The timing is

Rows of lettuce at Hillview Farm

tricky for this and we often get our plants ready too soon and watch them grow too tall and leggy. A stout compact plant will move more easily than an overgrown one.

About two weeks before your magic date start moving the flats outside. On day one leave them out for a few minutes on a warm afternoon. Choose a sheltered place protected from wind. On day two they can stay a little longer. Each day increase the time, paying attention to outdoor weather conditions. Above all don't forget them. If you come home from a shopping expedition that lasts too long you can find your tomatoes dried out, wind and sun-burned and falling over. This is not hardening-off but killing-off.

Transplanting is safer on a cloudy, still day. If you must do it on a sunny, windy day wait until the noon-heat is past and if possible protect each tomato or pepper plant with a little house of its own. This house can be a paper bag, a jar, etc.

Transplanting is a traumatic experience for any plant. You can minimize the shock if you plant in individual wee pots made of peat. They can go directly into the garden to break down as the plant grows. Water an hour before you plan to move the plants and water again when they are firmed into their new locations. Adding a seaweed fertilizer (made from liquid seaweed concentrate) to this first watering after a move helps to reduce the root shock.

Each year in July I wish I had thinned my carrots more in early June. It is difficult to convince yourself that every other one of those hopeful little 2 to 3 in. plants should be sacrificed. You are aiming for plants spaced 1 in. apart. If you don't do this you will have stunted, twisted small carrots. Other root crops which may require thinning are parsnips, turnips, kohlrabi and beets.

A later kind of thinning is called eating. You can pull out the small delicious carrots and eat them, at the same time giving their space to neighbouring carrots. This kind of thinning works well for fast-maturing crops like radish, lettuce and spinach.

Beets, often overlooked by the gardener planting in May, are one of the easiest crops to grow. Each seed put into the ground will sprout three or four plants. All but one of these should be snipped off with scissors. In about a month you can thin again by eating some of the tiny beets, leaves and all. Then continue eating beets all summer and late into the fall. They'll just sit there waiting looking red and green and healthy. Cylinder-shaped beets are an old-fashioned type that have become popular again. They sit high out of the ground but stay tender and don't get woody.

Now that the summer garden is started we need to deal with the idea that gardening is a lot of work. Maybe. But so is running or weight-lifting or aerobics or working out on a variety of machines.

Gardening also makes you hot and exposes you to ultraviolet rays. True. But what if someone asked you to labour in the hot sun chasing a tiny ball around an open field trying to knock it into a tiny hole?

Some people see a garden as a war zone, the enemy as frost that strikes in the night, as wind or hail or rain or drought, or creatures as tiny as an aphid or as big as a groundhog or white-tail deer, where blight or fungus or rot or moth and rust doth corrupt. Well, herein lies the challenge, the game of chess. Do you want to play or don't you?

Gardening compared to golf or weight-lifting or aerobics or running is an inexpensive sport. Your shoes won't need to be air-inflated state-of-the-art acquisitions; in fact the older the better. A straw hat is

Garden helpers must wear hats.

A flowering carrot.

the only de rigueur item for your exercise apparel. With a shovel and a rake and a spade you have a starter's set of gear.

A recent study by the Canadian Fitness and Lifestyle Research Institute concluded that two out of three Canadians are so physically inactive that it poses a health risk equivalent to smoking a pack of cigarettes a day. Lack of exercise contributes directly to heart disease, depression and osteoporosis. One hour of light exercise a day could make an important difference to the 63% of Canadians living sedentary lives.

Gardening is good exercise. It is usually done in warm weather which is helpful to muscles and bones. To avoid the extreme heat of the day, gardeners usually appear on the scene early in the morning or take advantage of the long summer evenings. When you do find yourself still planting, thinning or weeding in the noon-day sun, make sure you are wearing a wide-brimmed hat and a long-sleeved shirt and a good sun screen. As a gardener's skin is exposed to excessive hours of sun it becomes more imperative each year to take precautions.

Honestly the battle can be fun. More fun if you are winning. Now in May is a good time to prepare strategy. How will you deal with potato bugs, aphids, slugs and cabbage butterflies without resorting to chemicals? Can you outwit the ground hog without resorting to a gun? Now is a good time to read up on the slug baits and sticky traps and plant covers that we will try later.

One defence we can ready now is companion planting. There is evidence from studies that carrots and tomatoes love and protect each other, that nasturtiums planted next to turnips will keep away black flea beetles, that mint gives off an aroma attractive to parasitic wasps, that catnip and tansy can repel squash bugs.

A flower in a vegetable garden is more than just a pretty face. It can defend your vegetables. Its nectar can attract tiny parasitic wasps to prey on your garden pests. Because these wasps are so tiny they need tiny flowers; the trick is to get them blooming early before aphids or beetles or leaf-hoppers devour your crops.

The carrot family, the mint family and the daisy family all have flowers attractive to beneficial insects. Dill forms an umbel of tiny flowers just 45 days after planting. Coriander, which seeds itself year after year in my garden, is another fast-flowering umbel. Sweet alyssum also flowers quickly. As a border along your vegetable garden it will be doing more than just looking beautiful.

From personal experience I recommend "escape planting" for tomatoes which may suffer from fusarium or verticillium wilt, from septoria leaf spot or from early blight. These diseases over-winter in the soil and appear next year as leaves turning yellow (wilt) or as spotted leaves which wither and die (leaf spot or early blight). The recommended way to deal with this soil-borne infection is to plant tomatoes in a different spot each year, not coming back to the infected site for four years. You can also help the situation by buying or growing varieties that are resistant to the disease. These are labelled in the greenhouse, "F" to indicate fusarium wilt resistance and "V" to show resistance to verticillium wilt. You can also help by planting in full sun with good drainage and generous space between plants and in soil which is organically rich with nutrients.

Keeping tools and containers clean also helps guard against disease in the garden. By the time we have emptied our home-grown flats and pots bought from the greenhouses or given to us by friends, our garage or garden shed is likely a mess. On a sunny day I haul everything out on the lawn and wash it with the hose and a spray nozzle, let it dry in the sun and pack it all away, resolved to garden without mess the rest of the summer.

Having a cupboard in the garage or a shed near the garden helps. Have pegs and hooks to hang up tools, a place for muddy boots and gloves. I use several pairs of gloves and when they all get muddy I wash them in a pail and dry them on the grass.

One of my best garden tools is a piece of sturdy foam for kneeling on. This is better than knee pads because you only have one piece to try to not lose. Another wonderful item is a weeding trowel with a yellow handle. When you finish weeding you can see where you left it. With a brown handle you haven't a hope.

While we wait for August tomatoes, what can we eat from the garden in May? Spinach, lettuce, radish, dandelions from the lawn.

Some of these wildflowers are edible and will appear on the
dining table at Sooke Harbour Inn on Vancouver Island.

After gardening a while the lines between vegetable and flower and weed become blurred. Vegetables are things you eat; flowers are things you admire; weeds are things you pull and discard. But sometimes you can eat the flowers and sometimes you eat the weeds.

I had a good friend named Blanche Garrett who wrote books about wild foods. One day she phoned me to ask if I had any chickweed in my garden. I said facetiously that I didn't allow weeds in my garden. She said she'd be willing to bet I had some somewhere and she needed it for the cover of her new book. "OK, come and look."

Blanche found her chickweed (my chickweed) - "a creeping plant with a weak stem, with small, pointed, oval-shaped leaves opposite each other, and tiny white flowers shaped like stars set near the top of each branch." [2] It appears as "Chickweed and Orange Salad" on the lusciously green cover of her book, *A Taste of the Wild.*[2]

I am recalling Blanche and her chickweed just now because I have been reading news reports about genistein, a substance which seems to block the growth of new capillaries that supply some tumours, and seems to deter the proliferation of cancer cells. Genistein is found in the urine of people who eat soy beans and chickweed.

Dr. James Duke, a retired USDA enthnobotanist writing in *Organic Gardening* says that many farm and garden weeds are "nutritionally and medicinally superior to the crops with which they compete!"[3] He tosses chickweed into his spring salad for the genistein it contains as well as the saponin which is also being studied as a weapon against tumours.

If you make the leap to eating weeds, they will provide you with early garden greens before your own

Diary: I was too busy in May to write anything down, but later from the hot peace of July I could remember May: dandelions to dig, last year's dead growth to rake off the crown vetch, sod creeping into the garden to cut out, poppies to move from their seedbed by the compost to various locations, seedlings to carry inside and out and water and protect from wind, trips to garden stores, friends to exchange with, containers to find, what to put in containers this year, hoses to haul out of the basement, lawn cuttings to mix with last year's leaves in a compost pile, manure to spread. For a gardener May is the month which never has enough days.

crops are in the ground. They were planted by nature the year before. There is chickweed appearing in the garden you dug up in the fall, there are dandelions appearing on the lawn (eat the new-formed leaves), violets in the flower garden (eat the flowers), lamb's quarters in the meadow (eat the leaves). Wild garlic, believed to help prevent hypertension and heart ailments may grow in your neighbourhood. Use a plant guide for identification and be sure you are eating what you think you are from an area which is not sprayed and not along a roadside contaminated by traffic emissions.

When *Organic Gardening* magazine publishes an article on weed control, readers write in saying they eat them. One reader harvests lamb's quarters to sell at a farmers' market for 50 cents a bunch. Another loves purslane in soups and salads. Purslane is considered a nuisance in most gardens but this reader sees it as a source of omega-3 fatty acids, beta-carotene and vitamin E.

Spinach is cold-tolerant and easy to grow in the early spring. It is extremely high in iron and high in vitamins A, C, magnesium and potassium. It might not be good for people with arthritis or kidney stones.

SPINACH SALAD
bunch of spinach
bunch of lettuce
10 - 15 white mushrooms
¼ lb. bacon

Dressing:
juice of 1 lemon or 3 tbsp. juice
½ cup salad oil
2 tsp. sugar (or Splenda for diabetics)
1 tsp. salt
½ tsp. dry mustard
1 tsp. chopped onion
⅛ tsp. pepper
Wash vegetables and dry in spinner or on towel. Break spinach and lettuce into small pieces and slice mushrooms. Mix dressing ingredients and pour over vegetables just before serving. Makes large salad for 8 to 10 people.

SPINACH STRAWBERRY CHICKWEED SALAD
bunch of spinach
chickweed (when available)
strawberries, sliced

Dressing:
⅓ cup white sugar
½ cup oil
¼ cup white vinegar
2 tbsp. sesame seeds
2 tbsp. poppy seeds
2 tsp. minced onion
½ tsp. Worcestershire sauce
¼ tsp. paprika

BROCCOLI SALAD
5 cups broccoli chopped
½ cup raisins
¼ cup red onion chopped
2 tbsp. sugar
3 tbsp. vinegar
1 cup mayonnaise
10 bacon slices cooked
1 cup sunflower seeds
Chop broccoli, add raisins and chopped onion. Mix sugar, vinegar and mayonnaise to make dressing; pour over broccoli mixture. Just before serving crumble cooked bacon into small pieces and add along with sunflower seeds.

Early summer
garden and
landscape.

CHAPTER 6

JUNE

GARDENS OF EDEN

Agriculture, the landscape that surrounds us, is the rest of the story of the garden.
Douglas Chambers [1]

If the Garden of Eden ever exists in Canada, it exists in June. June is that moment in time when all flora is either just breaking into bloom or green and lush with the promise of bloom tomorrow. Every blossom is beautiful. Every leaf is soaking up the sun and the rain. Garden fauna are in a similar state of ecstasy, bees and butterflies as active as the day is long, birds feeding their young and animals everywhere enjoying the fat of the land.

In June we should all be living off the fat of the land, preferably our own land. For me, the symbol, the badge of June is a strawberry. For several years when our children were small, we grew strawberries. When we had too many, the children set up a stand on the front lawn and sold them. Neighbour kids joined them and they all learned something about selling as well as about the growing and weeding and picking. They thought it was the greatest fun, better than playing store - this was real!

When we don't have our own patch we can usually find a u-pick close to home. I go to one that has lots of weeds between the rows, evidence that the plants are not being sprayed with chemicals. This farm's berries are not the largest in the region but the flavour is great.

U-pick gardens are a bond between city and country. There is more involved than just getting some berries - there's the pleasure of being out in a field early in the morning on the best morning of the year, of showing small children how berries grow and watching them learn to pick. There's the tradition that two or three generations go out to do this together. Often I hear people in the next row talking about the farm they grew up on, the strawberries or raspberries or apples they picked when they were kids. There are memories available on a u-pick farm that can't be found in the city.

There is a unique satisfaction to be had by using foods in season. Pumpkin pie, even if made from a can, tastes a lot better in October than in June. It may have something to do with colour; the colour orange which I dislike the rest of the year seems to fill the very air in October - and is beautiful! When in June, eat strawberries. Eat lettuce and spinach and radishes and snow peas and green onions fresh from the garden. Don't buy from the supermarket what you can easily grow yourself. Just the excuse to go out there and pick is worth a lot.

From now until November it should be possible to eat "from hand to mouth" directly from garden to table. The advantage to your family will be fresh-tasting food, the best supply of vitamins and a sense of being in step with nature.

There is a special joy in using real unprocessed food, in creating from scratch. In each of us there is some memory of a grandmother who cooked naturally, bringing in an arm load of whatever was ready in the garden, adding some herbs and spices to the pot, disdaining recipes or writing them as a pinch of salt, a chunk of butter, a small teacup of milk.

I have discovered the joy of washing out my crisper on the first of July and leaving it empty, getting what I want directly from the garden. At first we eat lettuce, spinach, radishes and green onions, then beans, carrots, beets. Then the zucchini multiply and magnify and the kohlrabi are ready and the cucumbers and tomatoes and squash and melons ripen and finally the potatoes and pumpkins and turnips tell us it is Thanksgiving and Hallowe'en and will soon be Christmas.

Food is basic to life and health and the question of where it comes from becomes increasingly important. We can never have total control over what goes into our ground. If you buy produce in the store and toss the tops or peelings into your compost you are adding whatever pesticide residue is on the vegetable or fruit. But by growing and using your own most of the time you are gaining a lot of control.

56

Diary, June 4: Trying a new-to-you plant makes gardening more fun. My new plant this year is Stevia, an import from Paraguay, where the dried, crushed leaves have been used for centuries to sweeten food. Its sweetening capacity far exceeds sugar and it is being tested in the United States as a substitute for sugar. Since we have a diabetic son this plant is of particular interest to our family. I will plant Stevia in a container so it can be moved inside in September as it is not winter-hardy in Canada. In August its bloom will be small white flowers.

Home-grown does not have to mean your own back yard. If you live in a city without a back yard you can be part of a community garden. This can be a group of people banding together to rent a plot of land where each family can go to plant, weed and harvest their rows. Or it can be a demonstration garden where persons dedicated to promoting sustainable green space experiment and learn as they grow a garden.

Local food production can play a part in poverty relief. Educating or retraining mothers and fathers to feed their children directly from gardens is helpful to people who have lost their jobs or have to deal with pay cuts.

In connection with community gardens, collective kitchens have been set up in several cities, usually in churches or other community buildings. In Peterborough, members meet near the end of the month when family money is often scarce. Using $50 supplied by the church mission committee, they plan a shopping expedition and cook up two casseroles, soup, a salad such as cole slaw and school lunch goodies. In summertime what they cook up often comes directly

Digging a community garden in Peterborough, Ontario

from the community garden. Volunteer Kim Naish says, "We're not doing it for them, we're all doing it together and we learn from each other."

Winnipeg school children plant in the spring and harvest in the fall with parents helping to weed and water all summer. Their bumper crops of carrots and beets and turnips and potatoes go to the Winnipeg Food Bank. There are a dozen such school and church plots in the city. The largest of these contributed 363 kg (800 lb.) of vegetables.

Whether your garden is in the back yard or in an ecology park, June is a good time to look at a particular plant and study it. It's a bit like bird-watching except

that the plant won't fly away just when you get it into focus. Few plants are as interesting as the bean. It's the seed you put in a dish with a wet paper towel to show a child how a seed sprouts. It's the Jack-and-the-beanstalk story. It's the one that looks so good poking up through the earth in May. It's the one with a special mechanism to actually produce - not just use up - nitrogen; a mechanism common to all legumes.

Bacteria on the roots of beans and all legumes can pull nitrogen from the atmosphere, converting it to nitrate ions which can be used by the plant. In return the plant shares its sugars with the bacteria in a symbiotic relationship. From a gardener's point of view this looks like getting something for nothing. We've been led to believe that what we grow can be only as good as the soil we provide but here is a plant able to find its own nitrogen from the air!

Beans and peas can improve your soil if you turn the plants under when you finish harvesting. Or mow them off leaving the root nodules in the soil for other plants to use next year. Other legume crops can be grown specifically to add 'green manure' to your garden. Good choices are fast-growing crops like Dutch white clover, rye grass, buckwheat or alfalfa which can be planted in late summer or early fall and ploughed under next spring before garden planting time. Clover's ability to bring minerals to the surface making them available for other plants makes it a good choice. Rye grass grows quickly and is easy to till into the soil in the spring. Buckwheat, an old favourite green manure crop, attracts bees. Alfalfa has remarkable power to reach several feet deep into the earth bringing up nutrients not otherwise available to the garden, breaking up hard-packed earth, aerating the soil and improving its water retention. It is even possible to plant a fast crop in early spring and turn it under two or three weeks before planting vegetables. Or leave it there; just dig out a narrow row of the clover (throw it in your compost) and plant seeds in the row and you have a live mulch so you won't have to weed. For transplants you can dig a round hole in the clover leaving the rest of your cover crop intact.

During the summer whenever crops are harvested and ground becomes 'empty', green manure can be put in. Last year when I pulled up the bean rows in August, I planted white clover. It quickly formed a green carpet keeping weeds out and adding nitrogen to the soil. These cover crops help prevent erosion, improve the

A trellis helps beans grow like Jack's beanstalk.

soil structure, keep weeds down and ultimately replenish the soil with nitrogen.

A garden in the country knows no bounds. Its summer vines can run rampant into the pasture, its seeds can scatter and grow phlox and poppies and asparagus along the fence row. And the gardener may have a hard time to contain his/her own self. It is tempting to manage just a little more of that larger landscape which surrounds us. I find myself tending the red clover that grows in the hay field adjacent to my garden. The clover and I have our own symbiotic relationship: it flourishes because of runoff from my manured garden; I find clumps of it in my spring garden and move them to the edges where they become gatekeepers to ward off the encroaching field grasses.

To the gardener the world of field crops is just another step - a small step into a big field. Cover crops like clover and buckwheat and rye grasses can be used in the garden or to claim a piece of field and convert it to a garden. In the field where we had parked a trailer, a patch of land was bare. Here I scattered alfalfa seed and now have a lush piece of alfalfa which I am hoping birds may spread through the pasture. At any rate I have a nitrogen crop to cut and add to the compost heap.

Along the road where salt and gravel kicked up by traffic make a poor lawn, we are experimenting with crown vetch at one end and white clover at the other. The question is whether it will be easier to keep dandelions out of these patches than out of a poor grass lawn.

Getting back to beans; the beginning gardener will probably find yellow or green snap beans (also called string beans or wax beans or bush beans) a happy choice. They produce abundantly for three weeks beginning about 60 days after seeding.

Pole beans are fun to grow if you don't mind providing a lattice or wooden frame with strings for the plants to climb. Broad or fava beans can tolerate cool weather which allows early spring planting. Pinto and black beans each need 100 frost-free days.

Clover as a garden cover crop.

Strawberry pickers near Ida, Ontario.

Strawberries have high amounts of vitamin C and potassium and add fibre to the diet. Feasting on strawberries is easy in June.

STRAWBERRY TEA BREAD

3 eggs
1 cup sugar
1 cup salad oil
1 tbsp. vanilla
2 cups flour
1 tsp. cinnamon
1 tsp. salt
1 tsp. baking soda
½ tsp. baking powder
1½ cups rolled oats
2 cups crushed strawberries, (frozen may be used but not in June)

Mix eggs, sugar, oil and vanilla. Sift flour, cinnamon, salt, baking soda, baking powder. Add oats. Add dry ingredients to egg and sugar mixture. Add crushed berries and mix. Bake in greased and floured loaf pans at 190°C (375°F) for 45 minutes. (Recipe is from Jill Patterson of Orleans, Ontario, passed down from her mother.).

STRAWBERRY APPLE BISCUIT

$1/3$ to $2/3$ cup sugar
3 tbsp. all-purpose flour
2 tsp. lemon rind
1 tsp. cinnamon
2 cups strawberries, fresh or frozen
2 cups chopped fresh apples
1 to 2 tbsp. lemon juice

Combine above ingredients and put in an 8 in. square dish. Bake 10 minutes at 205°C (400°F).

In a mixing bowl combine:

1 cup flour
3 tbsp. sugar
1 tsp. baking powder
¼ tsp. baking soda
¼ tsp. salt
3 tbsp. cold butter (cut into above mixture)
$2/3$ cup buttermilk (stir in with a fork)

Drop this mixture by spoonfuls onto hot fruit making six mounds. Bake 35-40 minutes at 190°C (375°F) until top is golden.

Out in the garden, beans are not there one moment and the next moment they are bean profusion, hanging yellow or green all along the row. They supply vitamins A, B-complex and C, chlorophyll, carbohydrates, calcium, phosphorus, copper and cobalt. Finding the first carrots big enough to carry to the kitchen and add to the supper beans is a summer milestone. But soon after this orange letter day we'll have abundant carrots to serve in salads or simmer with mint or dill or serve in casseroles.

BEAN AND CARROT DISH

4-6 medium carrots
¾ cup water
1 tsp. sugar
½ tsp. salt
½ tsp. dill weed
2 cups green or yellow beans
¼ cup Italian dressing

Scrub carrots. Cut into 2-in. strips. Wash beans and remove ends, then snap in two. Put water, sugar, salt, dill weed in saucepan. Cook 5 minutes. Drain. Add Italian dressing.

TOMATO BASIL BEAN SALAD

4 tomatoes
2 tbsp. chopped basil leaves
2 tbsp. chopped parsley
2 tbsp. chopped green onions
1 cup yellow beans, finely chopped
salt or garlic salt and pepper
2 tbsp. olive oil

Slice tomatoes, layer in dish, adding seasoning and herbs. Drizzle olive oil over each layer. Cover with saran wrap and marinate in refrigerator 15 minutes.

Levern and Lillian Wood in their large, well-watered garden near Peterborough.

CHAPTER 7

JULY

THE LONG HOT DAYS OF SUMMER

Who is this guy, Herb Garden, that you keep going to see?
My friend's husband.

In a true garden of Eden, rain from the sky would provide all the moisture needed by our plants. Sometimes it does and we can sit inside and watch it happen at happy intervals. But during July in Canada this is most unlikely. Hot weather quickly evaporates available water, leaving the soil parched and the plants wilted. Wind also removes water through transpiration.

In very hot dry weather it can be beneficial to water a garden every day. One inch of water will provide moisture to a depth of one foot. The favoured times of day for watering are early morning or evening to avoid fast evaporation.

Container gardening demands more frequent waterings than a regular garden. Most containers need to be watered every day, even twice a day if in direct sun. Last year at a cottage where plants must survive from one weekend to the next without water, I tried a container with a water storage compartment at the bottom, an air space above it and a wick to draw the water up when the plant became dry. It worked extremely well. In a stump where I planted petunias, I packed moss around the plants to conserve moisture when no one was there to water.

Newly planted gardens need to be kept damp at all times until the seeds have sprouted. The usual way to do this is with a sprinkler attached to a hose. As summer goes on and the garden grows there will be restrictions imposed by cities; often you can water only on alternate days.

My neighbour has a knack for finding water. Barrels sit in his garden collecting rain water. A trough runs directly from the eavestrough downspout on his house to another big barrel. A few years ago he ran a hose down to the pond behind our houses and installed a pump. Now he turns it on at 7 p.m. to water his own garden and the gardens of neighbours. I have been known to get wet while working in the garden after supper forgetting that I am a lucky gardener who gets automatic "rain" every evening at 7:00 pm.

Two-year-olds are enthusiastic waterers. You can benefit from their energy if you can harness it.

The city of Ottawa sells a plastic rain barrel made to fit under a downspout on your house. It has a childproof lid, a screen to catch leaves and debris and a brass hose-fitting to connect to your garden hose. Depending on the size you purchase, it catches and holds 180 to 225 litres (48 to 60 gal.) of natural soft water with which to water your gardens.

Apart from using sprinkler systems and collecting rain, a gardener can help by conserving whatever moisture is available, This is done by mulching - protecting the soil from evaporation. Mulch is a layer of something placed on the soil to conserve moisture and retard weed growth and, if the mulch is organic material, improve the soil.

There are many mulch choices: newspaper with grass clippings on top, hay, cocoa bean shells, straw, weeds pulled out of the garden (before they go to seed), wood chips, sawdust, rice hulls, peat moss. Hay should not be used because it contains seed heads. Wood chips and

sawdust are carbon-rich and tend to remove nitrogen from the soil in the process of breaking down, so use some nitrogen-rich material such as composted manure with them. Leaves are nature's most abundant mulch. Forest floors are carpeted with them. Again you are adding carbon and may need to balance this with a nitrogen source. As summer wears on you will have bean stalks or pea vines rich in nitrogen to use as compost-mulch. Planting a "green manure" crop

Plants like this Cleome benefit most from watering early in the day.

Linda Fairheller in her garden at Bloomsbury Herbs and Edible Flowers near Apsley, Ontario.

between the rows of vegetables protects the soil with a living mulch.

Straw is my favorite mulch, clean, easy to work with, weed-free and easily available in most locations. In Peterborough it is available from the Ecology Garden at $3 a bale. You might also see straw advertised in the newspaper and have the fun of driving out to a farm to get it.

I can hardly wait to put down my straw and be done with weeding. Once it is down the soil stays cooler, protected from the hot sun and drying winds. Eventually the straw will break down adding nutrients

Anise hyssop (Agastache foeniculum) at Bloomsbury Gardens. The edible flowers have a licorice flavour and can be served on ice-cream, atop a cake, in teas or salads. Bees love the violet flowers.

Purple coneflower (Echinacea purpurea) is now widely used to boost the body's resistance to infection. Plains Indians had many uses for it ranging from snakebite to toothache.

Fennel

Herbal teas can be made of chamomile (flowers), mint (leaves), valerian (roots), rose(hips), fennel (crushed seeds), thyme and rosemary (leaves). Pour boiling water over herbs and let sit 10 minutes. Consult a good herb book for possible negative effects and know exactly what you are brewing.

to the soil and improving its aeration. In the meantime it provides a clean, weed-free walkway between plants and a good feeling that my garden is tucked in, safe from extremes of weather.

When fall comes, mulch can extend the season by protecting roots and lower leaves from the cold. Left on over winter it can protect perennial herbs from devastating freezing and thawing.

Mulches such as straw, weeds and grass clippings have one disadvantage. They provide a safe haven for slugs. If slugs become a problem you might have to leave the ground bare for a season to get rid of them.

Herbs add wonderful new dimensions to a garden. Most bear small, colourful flowers. Many are loved for their tangy scents. Each of them has kept a place in generations of gardens because it has a specific purpose. Often this purpose is an incomparable flavour or the power to cure some ailment of mankind.

Finding chives in the garden soon after the snow melts means great flavour for salads or soups. But in July you can also enjoy their purple pom-pom flowers swaying in the breeze. Mint earns its place by the aroma it adds to the garden and the taste it adds to potatoes or meat or salads. If you grow peppermint (Mentha piperita) break off a few leaves, pour on hot water, let it steep and you have peppermint tea. By July mint is topped with flowers in purple or blue.

Bergamot is a member of the mint family with showy flowers in red or lavender or reddish purple. Its other names help to describe it: Bee Balm because bees are attracted to its nectar; Oswego Tea because the Oswego Indians made tea from its leaves. Its flavour has been described as a mix of mint and sage. Bergamot grows better if you dig it up every two years and replant it. It adds a great splash of colour to any garden.

Oregano is a favourite in the kitchen for spaghetti dishes, pizzas, sauces, soups and dressings. In the garden it contributes purple flowers. Pick these in their prime and they dry beautifully for flower arrangements - just hang upside down.

Dill's place in the pioneer garden was secured by its contribution to pickles. Dill produces umbels (parasol-like arrangements of flowers) atop long stalks. For pickles the heads should be picked before the flowers open fully. But long before the flowers appear we can use dill leaves in salads and casseroles. When the flowers do appear let some open and bloom adding a soft yellow glow to the garden. Plants bearing their flowers on umbels have another contribution: the nectar in their tiny flowers is particularly attractive to parasitic wasps which are needed to attack damaging garden bugs.

Plants develop ways to protect themselves against disease and this protection can often be transferred to humans. Aloe's juices are used to treat burns and cuts, sunburns and frostbite. Fennel can be healthful for asthmatics. Garlic is a powerful drug believed to ward off numerous infections. Valerian is useful as a sedative and anti-depressant. Feverfew is helpful to some migraine sufferers.

An estimated 2500 plants have been used for medicinal purposes but only a handful of these have been scientifically studied. As powerful healers, herbs need to be used with caution. Before eating large amounts of any herb it is wise to know what it is capable of doing. Parsley, which is a great source of iron and vitamins and chlorophyll may speed up the heart in some people. Several herbs - hyssop, parsley in large doses - are to be avoided by pregnant women because of possible miscarriage. Comfrey is used

Herb garden at Bloomsbury.

Herbes de Provence (brought back from Provence by a vacationing friend):
2 cups savory   1 cup thyme
1½ cup oregano   1 cup basil
1½ cup marjoram   ½ cup rosemary
Mix all herbs together and bottle for family and friends.

externally to heal cuts and bruises, even to aid bone-healing, but recent research suggests it should not be taken internally as it contains carcinogenic alkaloids.

Many herbs are beautiful before they flower by virtue of their foliage. Fennel is tall and feathery, its taste a licorice flavour that kids love. Parsley is velvety green with shapely leaves and a flavour that enhances almost anything you cook. Basil is dainty out in the garden and a culinary joy in the kitchen; all tomato dishes crave basil, it is good in salads, in meat dishes, in salad dressings and sauces.

In a diverse garden the distinction between vegetable and flower becomes blurred. In July everything wants to flower and even weeds are beautiful. Peas are producing dainty white or pink or red blossoms. Beans are flowering in colours that range from white and purple to the red of Scarlet Runner or the pink of Sunset. Early broccoli will soon shoot those jaunty yellow flowers. Cucumber and zucchini and squash and pumpkins produce flowers bold enough to rival an orchid and make a bee dizzy with delight.

Diary, July 5: Tomato upstarts tend to appear all over my garden, gifts from the compost pile. Most of these are treated as weeds and discarded. But a few which grow in convenient places and have a hardy look are allowed to remain for late-season tomatoes. If your garden lacks upstarts you can start additional tomatoes in June by cutting 8-inch shoots from healthy plants. Put these in pots in a shady place and water well. In two weeks they will be ready for a sunny location in the garden and will give you extra tomatoes in September.

In July there is no escaping the attack of the giant zucchini. There they are, tiny wee fruit one day and enormous demanding hulks the next. Most of us have learned to keep our planting down to two plants after one summer when they were out of control. Do you live in a neighbourhood where people lock their cars to avoid finding giant zucchini in the back seat?

But joking aside, zucchini is a wonderful base for many tasty dishes. Each year about February I wish I had saved more of it in my freezer. I have the same problem with rhubarb. These two gifts of nature are so abundant in season that we can't fully appreciate them until they are gone. Frozen zucchini goes into muffins or breads or thickens soups or makes casseroles. If you have lots of time in the summer you can make casseroles ahead in oven-proof dishes. When frozen, the casserole can be slipped out of the dish and stored in a freezer bag. Or throw zucchini chunks into the food processor, then store the grated zucchini in small portions ready for muffins or favourite bread recipes. These small portions work well for soup, too. I also like to slice zucchini when they are about three inches in diameter and store in freezer bags. The slices can be separated with a knife before they begin to thaw, then spread in a casserole dish. If you are really short of time throw the whole zucchini in a bag and microwave it briefly to thaw next winter.

Meanwhile in July the arrival of zucchini coincides with a garden full of herbs. Using zucchini as a base and herbs to enhance the flavour, we can be creative and serve up a dish of summer any day in July or all year if we use the freezer.

ZUCCHINI CASSEROLE

2 cups zucchini, sliced
I cup grated cheese
5 slices cooked and crumbled bacon (optional)
$^1/_3$ cup onion, chopped
I to 2 tsp. chopped fresh oregano
I to 2 tsp. chopped fresh basil
salt and pepper to taste
2 large tomatoes sliced or 8oz. tomato sauce
¼ cup parmesan cheese
I to 2 slices of bread crumbled
I to 2 tbsp. butter

Arrange half the zucchini in bottom of dish. Add half of cheese, bacon, onion, herbs, tomatoes or tomato sauce. Repeat for second layer. Melt butter in frying pan, stir in bread crumbs. Put on top of casserole. Sprinkle parmesan on top. Bake at 180°C (350°F) for 30 minutes.

Zucchini

FRYPAN ZUCCHINI

This is a very loose recipe which says if you have a zucchini you can add whatever else your garden provides and produce a quick supper veggie.

zucchini slices
I in. of water and a dab of butter
I medium onion, chopped
½ pepper, chopped
tomatoes, peeled and cut into pieces
fresh herbs: basil, oregano, parsley
carrots, celery; pears or other fruit
barbecue or chili or tomato sauce
ketchup or salsa
grated cheese sprinkled on top

Use whatever you have. Simmer the zucchini and onions as you prepare and add the other vegetables. Add the grated cheese when supper is ready.

CHOCOLATE ZUCCHINI BREAD

3 eggs
2 cups white sugar
I cup oil
3 tbsp. cocoa
2 cups zucchini, grated
I tsp. vanilla
3 cups all-purpose flour
I tsp. cinnamon
I tsp. salt
I tsp. baking soda
I½ tsp. baking powder

Beat eggs, sugar, oil. Add cocoa, zucchini and vanilla. Mix dry ingredients and add to wet. Bake in two loaf pans at 180°C (350°F) for 60 minutes.

Chickens at Hillview Farm.

CHAPTER 8

AUGUST
A FINE BALANCE OF BUGS

*Gardening is a very fine thing, because you get such an unmistakable
answer as to whether you are making a fool of your-self, or hitting the mark.*
Goëthe [1]

If you were born after World War II and learned to garden with synthetic chemicals you might indeed feel like a fool when you "go off drugs" and produce puny carrots and bug-eaten beans. Chemical fertilizers which feed the plants get fast-growing results but destroy the complex soil community leaving it vulnerable to disease, erosion and drought. Herbicides which kill weeds, fungicides which control disease and insecticides which kill insects are all powerful and effective weapons. But like all weapons their potential for killing extends beyond their intended target.

When you go "on the organic wagon" your garden suffers withdrawal symptoms. It will take one or two or three years to re-establish the millions of micro-organisms per tablespoon of soil which provide growing power and protect plants from disease. Nitrogen, phosphorus, potassium, carbon, hydrogen, oxygen, calcium, magnesium, sulphur, boron, copper, iron, manganese, molybdenum, zinc and chlorine are all present in healthy soil. You can help re-establish these nutrients by supplying plenty of manure that first year.

Animal waste by whatever name you call it, comes with abundant microorganisms already at work. If you can locate an organic farmer willing to sell you manure, you know you have a good product free from unnatural chemicals. Your own compost is great stuff, too, but it is difficult to make enough until you have bountiful growth under way.

Nature's balance is a precarious thing, especially in a garden which is, after all, a man-made interference with whatever nature provided in this location. There will be times, particularly in the three years of transition from "chemical" to "organic" gardening, when the bad bugs seem to outnumber the good. The few hardy bad guys who survived in spite of chemical warfare in gardens up and down the street will rush joyously into your garden when you quit using the poisons. The good guys who went off to hedge rows and other unsprayed places will come back to your garden and eat the bad guys but it may take a little time. Until these troops arrive you will feel you are losing the war.

By August you will know what the bad guys are eating but you might not know who they are. If you are a bird-watcher you may have developed habits of observation which you can now turn on the bugs. Does it have one stripe or two? Is it orange or yellow, one centimetre or two centimetres in length? Expert bug-watchers advise carrying a notebook to the garden to write down what you observe: what bugs appear to be eating the plant, time of year they appear, what controls them, what does not work, whether there are fewer than last year.

Hand-picking bugs has two advantages. It gets rid of the bug when you see it and it lets you identify the enemy. You can keep a glass jar handy and take it inside to check against a book. A bug book with lots of illustrations is a good investment. Pictures should be in colour since exact hues are an important aid to identification. (See recommended book list, page 117.)

Neighbours can be valuable allies in your bug wars. They are likely dealing with the same pests. They and members of your garden club will come up with ingenious solutions which you can try. My 78-year-old neighbour swats cabbage butterflies with a badminton racquet. Mary Perlmutter uses diatomaceous earth (DE) to control slugs and snails. DE is made up of the fossilized shells of algae called diatoms. Diatoms have sharp projections which pierce an insect's cuticle causing it to die of dehydration. DE will also kill beneficials so it should be used sparingly, e.g. around cabbages susceptible to cabbage maggot.

Sticky traps are an easy way to decrease the pest population in your garden. Use one tablespoon of petroleum jelly and one tablespoon of liquid dish-washing soap. For house plants and indoor herbs infested with whitefly apply to small strips of yellow cardboard. For outside it is necessary to use pieces of wood, preferably painted yellow. The flies are attracted to yellow.

Commercial products are also available with names like Tangletrap or Tanglefoot or Stickem. The sticky fly-coils which have been used for years in farm kitchens to trap houseflies, work in the garden too.

Another approach is to give the beetles and maggots and slugs something better than your plants. Put a nice fat carrot into the ground near your seedling if wireworms are a problem. Twice a week pull up the bait carrot and dispose of the wireworms. The same trick will work with onion maggots - just bury a mature onion with your dutch sets and let it attract any adults that are laying eggs. Leave a damaged tomato lying on the ground and check it early in the morning; you may find slugs feasting on it.

Earwigs can be trapped by using a piece of pipe or hose. They like dark hiding places. Or put a small plastic dish in the ground, its rim at soil level. For bait use some oil from a can of salmon or tuna. Earwigs are not necessarily bad. In a garden they eat many small pests and good-soldier bugs will usually keep their numbers down anyway.

Sometimes, due to human activity, nature gets out of balance. A friend tells me he went out every morning to collect and kill earwigs in his garden and record the daily kill on his calendar. When their total reached 10,000 he quit recording.

A more sophisticated trapping approach involves pheromones - sex chemicals which attract insects to mates. Synthetic pheromones in special traps can capture male insects before they mate. Commercial traps are available to hang in fruit trees collecting codling moth and cherry fruit flies and peach tree borers.

There are two ways to deal with slugs and snails: repel them or attract them. Ginger or three-inch pieces of fresh-cut fennel helps keep them away. Crushed limestone spread around plants is effective because it pierces their skin. Or use wood ashes which kills slugs by drying their slimy film.

Using the other approach you can attract and destroy them by sinking a can or pie plate to the brim and filling it with beer or a mixture of one tablespoon molasses or sugar and one tablespoon yeast in water with a little cooking oil around the top. Or keep the empty orange or grapefruit halves from breakfast to set out in the garden cut side down. Each morning nab the slugs and snails you find under the orange or grapefruit. Another trick is to give them a board to hide under, then check each day and destroy the dwellers you find. I have used a stack of black plastic flowerpots to hold up the row cover which protects my broccoli from white butterflies which would lay eggs on the leaves. Slugs make the mistake of hiding under these by day so I find them and destroy them.

In my tomato patch however, slugs are the winners this year. My tomatoes are too crowded and too close to squash plants which provide big leaves for slugs to hide under. Next year the tomatoes will be better spaced.

Slug on tomato

To catch slugs fill a small dish or can with a mixture of yeast and sugar in water.

In August you are dealing with the enemy face to face but having seen the whites of their eyes this year you can consider prevention for next year. First and foremost you must have good soil to produce healthy plants able to withstand pest and disease organisms. Research shows that as plants become unhealthy they become more attractive to pests as their turgor pressure drops. The normal distention and resiliency of their living tissue lessens as they approach the wilt point, making it easier for pests to attack.

Crop rotation is an important defence against disease because organisms which attacked your tomatoes last year will over-winter in the soil to attack again this year. But if you practice rotation your tomatoes will be on the other side of the garden safely out of reach. As much as possible juggle your carrots and cabbage and squash and tomatoes so nothing grows where it grew last year.

Try to choose seeds of plants that are resistant to disease. Heirloom plants (old-fashioned varieties) are becoming popular as gardeners realize that they often have built-in resistance to disease and pests, an example of survival of the fittest occurring through the centuries.

Companion planting is another preventive trick. Some companion plants act as a trap crop by attracting insects away from your crop: nasturtiums can lure flea beetles away from cabbage seedlings. Others serve their neighbours by repelling certain pests: catnip and tansy to repel squash bugs; rosemary and sage to repel cabbage maggot; thyme, dill or marigold to keep white butterflies away from cabbage and broccoli; radish to repel cucumber beetles. But more often companion plants work by attracting insects beneficial to another plant.

Every day in your garden beneficial insects are re-enacting the Battle of Britain. Fast, effective, often invisible, they swoop down on the enemy insects and larvae and take them out. Encourage them by providing landing strips and fuelling stations; many of them require nectar and pollen as well as larvae for their diet. Parasitic wasps are attracted to the tiny umbrel flowers of dill, fennel, coriander, hyssop, lemon balm, rosemary, caraway, Queen Anne's lace, mint, lovage, parsley, thyme and yarrow. They will lay more eggs if they eat nectar from these flowers first. The eggs will hatch as parasites on the caterpillars and larvae that are eating your plants.

Predator insects such as lacewings and hover flies will also visit flowers for the pollen they provide, then stay around to eat aphids, cutworms, bean beetles, leafhoppers, and tomato hornworm larvae. Larger predators such as paper wasps, ladybugs, ground

Praying mantis nymphs eat aphids and leaf-hoppers. Adults attack any insect they can catch, even each other.

Sunflowers provide large landing pads for the predatory insects needed to control garden pests.

beetles and rove beetles prefer larger flowers, so give them sunflowers, daisies or purple coneflower. These are composites with petals arranged around a large pollen centre - a perfect landing pad for an airborne insect.

Since my garden grows on the edge of a natural meadow (not tilled for 30 years) I have access to clover and alfalfa plants which I encourage around the garden. Because of the garden's fertility, these plants do much better near the garden than in the rest of the field. An expanse of crown vetch near our garden flowers all summer and attracts a multitude of insects as well. Small quantities of buckwheat, clover, alfalfa or crown vetch can be purchased at agricultural stores and planted around your garden. Even grasses are beneficial as they harbour predatory bugs.

Another approach is to buy and release beneficial insects. Many gardeners, myself included, have purchased a thousand lady beetles and released them in the garden only to have them 'run away home'. In my case home was probably the large natural meadow which offered a more diverse menu than my limited garden. If lady beetles do take up residence in your garden they will eat aphids and mealybugs and spider mites. You can also buy predatory mites to control spider mites or beneficial nematodes which are parasitic against root weevils, corn rootworms and many other garden pests. These nematodes also work to decompose organic material so you likely already have them in your mound of compost. Rove and ground beetles can be encouraged by having stones or boards or mulch in the garden providing the shelter they like.

Getting to know the insects in your garden requires a lifetime of observation. Perhaps the best advice about controlling insects in the garden is, "Be willing to relinquish control." Let nature find its own balance. Let some of the bad guys live; after all if you could kill them all you would leave nothing for the good guys to eat. Think of your garden as a place of abundance where there is enough for all of you, a garden of Eden where there is food for the snake and snail as well. Ninety per cent of all the insects you see are up to good, not evil. Remember also that the average healthy plant can have 30 percent of its bulk eaten by bugs and still survive.

If you must take drastic measures consider Bacillus thuringiensis (BT), a microbial biological pesticide which produces toxins to kill caterpillar pests. It is effective against cabbage loopers, tomato hornworms and coddling moth larvae among others. It should be used sparingly as it can kill larvae of butterflies you don't want to kill. There is also evidence that some insects you do want to kill have developed a resistance to it. The next least toxic weapon would be pyrethrum made from pyrethrum daisy flowers. Pyrethrum kills lady beetles along with the bugs you are targeting. It can also cause the symptoms of hay fever in some people.

Diagnosis of disease in the garden is often difficult. With careful observation and reference to books you can sometimes identify the disease. Moving plants to a different location next year may avoid fusarium wilt on your tomatoes. If it occurs late in the season you might only need to plan better strategy for next year. If a plant is badly diseased and you want to protect neighbouring plants, you can pull it up and dispose of it in a hot compost pile or in a sealed plastic bag in your household garbage.

Prevention of disease is easier than treatment:
1. Provide biologically vibrant soil.
2. Buy healthy plants.
3. Keep them watered.
4. Keep tools clean.
5. Rotate crops.

It is easier to work toward a happy balance of life on garden and farm if we know that such a balance existed almost everywhere until after World War II. By looking at the lives of parents or grandparents we can glimpse a rhythm of life more attuned to the earth.

My parents lived side by side in a small village south of Ottawa. His people were farmers; hers kept a village store. He was born in 1895, she in 1905. Both lived the first part of their lives without automobiles, electricity, telephone, television or shopping malls. They grew up in what some historians have dubbed the "Age of

Wild flowers and hanging basket containers at the Hunter farmhouse near Peterborough, Ontario.

Innocence" soon to be shattered by World War I, the Great Depression and World War II.

Dad, who became a storekeeper always remained part farmer at heart. From his memories a kind of Utopia emerges - a farm on the edge of a small village, a family of nine all working on the farm as they grew up. The farm was so self-sufficient that they only needed to buy sugar and tea and flour at the store. Farming was done with horses, using the intensive labour of a large family and crop rotation, no commercial fertilizer, herbicide or pesticide. Manure supplied the fertility . Dad could not remember pests ever being out of control. Their apple orchards produced a wide variety of apples - Russets were his favourite - without ever being sprayed. A maple bush provided the year's supply of maple syrup. The farm supplied meat, milk, butter and eggs. A large garden grew the potatoes and carrots and turnips and squash, the cucumbers and berries for pickles and jams that kept the family larder stocked all year.

1910. It's a picture of what was possible then. Some of it could be possible again.

A single toad will eat 1500 earwigs in a season according to research done at the Toronto Zoo. Toads will only stay in your garden if it is all-organic since their porous skin quickly absorbs any toxic chemical. They like mulch and bush plants to hide under, piles of rocks, commercial toad abodes or broken crockery, or even a board propped up on rocks in the shade.

Diary, August 4: This summer a snowball bush and I are fighting a battle with a new-to-us infestation of tiny caterpillars which are attacking viburnums in our area. They appeared in June. Because they make their way up from the ground I tried to stop them with sticky tape but I was too late and they ate all the leaves off the bush and no snowballs appeared. I expected the bush to die but a few weeks later the leaves miraculously reappeared. A friend warned me that the caterpillars would come back. They did but this time the tape stopped most of them and the bush looked reasonably good all summer. The problem is that these caterpillars overwinter in the soil and attack before my garden has a supply of predator wasps and bugs to control them. This year I plan to buy alyssum plants already flowering and plant them beside the snowball in hope of attracting an army of parasites. I will also put abundant compost around the bush in the hope of introducing parasitic nematodes to attack the over-wintering caterpillars. If this does not work I may have no snowballs again in June.

Beets are full of flavour and colour; they provide calcium, phosphorus, sodium, potassium, iron and magnesium as well as vitamins A, B-complex, C and folic acid. Some of their vitamins are lost as beets are cooked for 30-60 minutes depending on size. To keep all the vitamins, try a beet salad. If cooking beet greens, steam these separately for three to five minutes.

BEET-ONION-CELERY SALAD
4-6 beets, uncooked
1 onion, sliced in rings
2 stalks celery, cut in pieces
1 tbsp. lemon juice
1 tbsp. wine vinegar
1 tbsp. honey
salt, pepper
fresh basil
fresh parsley

Peel and grate the beets. (Use plastic gloves to avoid turning hands red.) Add onion and celery. Stir remaining ingredients together. Stir into beets. Cover. Put into refrigerator for 15 minutes before serving.

CORN ON THE COB needs no recipe, just a pot of boiling water. Shuck the ears and drop them in. Turn the heat off and leave the corn in the water for 3-5 minutes. Eat with butter and salt. Corn provides vitamins A, B and C, potassium, phosphorus, zinc, iron, magnesium and lots of fibre.

Tomatoes, cucumbers, lettuce and onions fresh from the August garden make this a best ever summer salad.

GREEK SALAD
3 tomatoes
2 cucumbers
½ head romaine lettuce in pieces
2 green onions
6 black olives
½ cup feta cheese
Dressing:
½ cup olive oil
¼ cup red wine vinegar or 2 tbsp. lemon juice
1½ tsp. oregano
⅛ tsp. garlic powder, salt and pepper

Toss salad ingredients in a bowl (except feta cheese). Shake dressing ingredients in a bottle until blended. Pour over salad, toss. Sprinkle feta cheese on top.

Round and cylinder-shaped beets grow easily in any garden.

In September vegetables move from gardens to kitchen counters.

CHAPTER 9

SEPTEMBER
MUTINY OF THE BOUNTY

I have often thought that if heaven had given me a choice of my position and calling, it should have been on a rich spot on earth, well-watered and near a good market for the production of the garden.
Thomas Jefferson [1]

If your garden was a success you might have it turn on you now. All those cucumbers, tomatoes, squash and pumpkins will suddenly ripen and demand your full attention just when the weather turns cranky, too.

It's getting colder. The vegetables want to be covered at night. Or they want to be picked, pulled, dug, harvested, washed, dried, carted into a garage or cellar or root house. Better still, they would like to be pickled, preserved, canned, frozen, made into relish or ketchup or casseroles or pies. You are only one person. You're under attack!

Tomatoes are probably our best-loved vegetables. No-one wants to lose any of the red beauties to cruel frost. There are three types of tomatoes which could be maturing in your August-September garden: large-fruited beef tomatoes about 10 cm in diameter; round medium-sized fruits about 5 cm across; cherry tomatoes which range from cherry sized to plum sized and are often grown in patio pots. Generally smaller tomatoes

ripen sooner than the big ones, but I am likely to have all three types still producing in September. In six-quart baskets and bowls, tomatoes of all sizes are carted into kitchens to be dealt with.

Every family has its favourite tomato recipes. Grandma's Chili Sauce. Aunt Beth's Tomato Ketchup. A simple way to deal with excess tomatoes is to cook, put into containers and freeze them to be used in soups or stews or on the table as a vegetable. Plunge the fruit into boiling water for 30 seconds, then into ice cold water for one to two minutes. Now the skin comes off easily. Plop them into the cooking pot. In my family stewed tomatoes are served hot in a soup bowl to which each person adds crackers, a bit of butter, salt, pepper and a bit of sugar. Delicious with any meal.

Spaghetti sauce is another favourite at our house. I fill a Dutch oven three-quarters full of tomatoes, then add 3 small onions or a big one, a green pepper, a clove of garlic, salt and pepper, 2 tbsp. vinegar, 1 tbsp. brown

Tomatoes, red on the vine.

the daytime temperature still rises to about 13°C. (55°F), your green tomatoes will continue to ripen. When the temperature begins to stay below 13°C (55°F) the game is over. Pick tomatoes that are full-sized and beginning to turn from deep green to pink. If all the ripening process takes place off the vine, the tomato will not develop the sugars and the vitamin C and the flavour you expect in a tomato.

If partially green tomatoes are put into a paper bag with an apple, the ethylene which the apple gives off helps to make the tomatoes ripen. If you want them to ripen slowly arrange them, not touching, on a shelf in a cool dark basement or garage where the temperature ranges from 13-16°C (55-61°F). When you want to speed the ripening process, move them into a warm kitchen with temperature 16-30°C (61-86°F).

If you have a lot of green tomatoes you can make green tomato relish or serve the family fried green tomatoes. Another solution is to pull the whole plant and hang it upside down in the shed or garage or basement with its load of green tomatoes still ripening.

This year I had a lot of green tomatoes in mid-September when we were going away for two weeks. In zone 5 you can count on one night of hard frost during the last two weeks of September so I pulled up the tomatoes, cages and all, tucked their roots into plastic bags and set them up on the garage floor. My little garden in the garage lasted for another month as the tomatoes ripened. By mid-October they were dropping leaves and looking messy; I picked the remaining tomatoes, spread them out on a table in the garage to ripen slowly, and tossed the plants out.

I usually have a few late plants of cherry tomatoes (upstarts from compost seeds) which grow along a southern brick wall. These survive frost until Hallowe'en

sugar, 1½ tsp. basil, 1½ tsp. oregano, small celery leaves, fresh parsley. Simmer 2 to 3 hours, then freeze in containers. When I use it later I add a can of tomato soup to thicken it, plus additional basil, oregano and garlic salt.

When really short of time there is another way to deal with ripe tomatoes. Wash them, put them into bags and pop them into the freezer. Later they will go into soup and stews or casseroles. This is the easiest way to deal with hundreds of cherry tomatoes. When making soup in January I find bags of wee tomatoes in the freezer and throw them unpeeled into the pot.

Not all the tomatoes in a September garden are red. The green ones are young hopefuls running out of time. If you cover them when a full moon threatens frost and when I pull them up and drape them over the wooden slats of a chaise longue (pad removed) in the garage. I can probably pick these tomatoes until Christmas or until a cold snap reaches into the garage and gets them.

Cucumbers are impatient September vegetables. If they have not already been turned into pickles or hot-dog relish there is very little time left. They can't stand the slightest frost and when you pick them they won't keep long. There is not much you can do to prolong the life of fresh cucumbers. They belong to the salad days of summer. The ones we buy in the supermarket all winter have been waxed in an attempt to preserve them but their taste is nothing like a crisp sweet summer cucumber. Just before that frosty night you'll pick the last of them and keep them in a cool place for as long as you can, but then it's over.

To use up the last of your cucumbers, try sautéing them for 2 or 3 minutes with green onions in 1 or 2 tbsp. of butter in a frypan. Add a dash of salt, pepper and sugar and sprinkle with dill weed or parsley. After the 3 minutes, you can add 1 or 2 sliced tomatoes and some basil and cook until just heated through.

If you have time you can always turn cucumbers into pickles. If you don't have time you can marinate cucumbers and keep them a week in the refrigerator. Mix 1 cup of water with ½ cup of vinegar, ½ tsp. salt and 1 tbsp. brown sugar. Heat to boiling. Slice cucumbers into a quart jar and pour the boiling liquid into the jar.

Beets are an easy vegetable to grow and can be harvested from July through September. At first you eat those baby beets with tender green leaves. Cook the beets until almost tender, then put the leaves on top so they steam-cook for 4 or 5 minutes or less. Don't peel beets before you cook them. Scrub and leave the skin

Cucumbers

and one inch of stem on to preserve the colour. When cooked, plunge the beet into cold water or hold under the cold water tap and slip the skin off in your hands.

Fresh summer beets need no embellishment; later you might try Harvard Beets by adding a sauce of 2 tbsp. cornstarch, $\frac{1}{3}$ cup sugar, ½ tsp. salt. Stir in ¼ cup vinegar and ½ cup beet water. Add beets and a dab of butter.

In summertime I save the juice of pickles and pop beets left over from dinner into the brine. Presto - beet pickles!

Sometime during August or September you may want to make a proper batch of beet pickles to enjoy next winter. Pull about four quarts of beets. Cut big beets into pieces, leave little ones whole and cook until tender, then remove skins. Meanwhile mix 3 cups vinegar, 2 cups water, 2½ cups sugar, 2 tsp. allspice, ½ tsp. whole cloves, 1 tsp. salt and a 3 inch stick of cinnamon and boil for 15 minutes. Add beets and simmer 5 minutes more. Pack beets into sterilized jars;

Lily Lake hot dog relish

bring the syrup to boiling again and pour over beets. Seal. Process jars 10 minutes in a boiling water bath.

Beet roots can survive the first frosts although the foliage will die. Leave a few in the ground to harvest throughout October. When you dig them you can store in wet sand or cook them up and freeze them. Next January put them frozen into the microwave or put them into the oven in a casserole dish with a dollop of butter when you are cooking a roast. Another great use for beets is making borsch either now or next winter using the frozen cooked beets.

Nothing in the September garden is as much fun as your first ripe cantaloupe. In zone 5 or 6 or even 7 a ripe cantaloupe is a green-thumb achievement. The average cantaloupe or honey dew melon would like four months of warm weather, but varieties developed for northern climates can ripen in 75 days or, given a hot summer, 65. Look for names like Earlisweet or Farnorth or Fastbreak.

I had attempted cantaloupe before in my zone 5 without success until I read that hills are the secret. Hills heat up faster in springtime; they also provide an extra depth of loose soil for those new roots to spread through. I shaped two heaps of earth, compost and manure and set out plants which had been started indoors in peat pots, then moved for a time to my computer-printer cold frame (a box with a hinged lid and plexiglass top which once housed a printer). Cantaloupes, honeydew melons and watermelons would like the temperature to be 21°C (70°F) when they go into the garden. They would like their earth heated up to 26°C (80°F). To achieve this, cover the hills with black plastic, cut slits for plants. If cold nights come along cover the plants with a blanket. Or you can use Kosy-coats (a circular wall of water in plastic tubes to hold heat against the frost).

In late August or early September when the cantaloupe is ready to eat, the skin turns from green to pale brown with a netted look. Best of all, there's the scent of ripe melon when you walk in the garden. Check the stem-to-melon connection; a ripe melon should slip away from the stem easily when ripe.

To decide when a watermelon is ripe look for a duller shine to the skin and a tendril near the stem

Help cantaloupes ripen faster: slide aluminum foil or aluminum trays underneath to reflect more solar rays onto the melons.

turning brown and curly. The skin where it sits on the ground will turn creamy yellow. If you rap on the melon with your hand a ringing sound means not ripe yet, a muffled sound means it is ready now.

Potatoes are not in a big hurry to get out of the ground although their foliage will disappear at 5°C (41°F). Dig when needed in the fall or just before freeze-up for winter storage.

Broccoli will keep producing in the cool fall garden and can even be picked wearing a cap of snow. Brussels sprouts will last in the garden for several weeks after the first frost. Or pull up the entire plant and hang it upside down in garage or basement and pick the sprouts when you like.

Other plants which do well in the cold are spinach, cabbage, kale and Swiss chard. Turnips and parsnips need cold weather. Leave turnips or rutabagas in until the soil begins to freeze to let their sugar content increase. Parsnips are best left in the ground covered with 50 cm (20 in.) of leaves. You can dig some in the January thaw or wait until April.

Carrots can remain in the ground all winter. Last year I left carrots in the garden, heaping leaves on top of the row. Until January I went out occasionally and dug them. Then other distractions or the depth of snow or maybe the cold north winds made me forget about them. When I started to spade up the garden I got a nice surprise - good spring carrots.

Only part of the row was good, the other half had frozen because the depth of leaves was not great enough. In zone 5 you need a good 50 cm (20 in.). You also need boards or branches to hold the leaves from blowing until they freeze. Be sure to pound in tall stakes at either end of the row or you will never find those carrots for Christmas dinner under all that snow.

As if it isn't enough to have all those vegetables calling for your September attention, there are herbs in your garden whose days are numbered and they would like to be saved. Basil is a great favourite of many cooks, sadly missed when the season is over. Herbs can be dried for winter use but much of the flavour is lost. There are other tricks you can try. Chop basil and put into ice-cube trays or plastic muffin tins, then cover with olive oil. To use some winter day place a paper towel on a plate, set the frozen cube on the towel and let the oil soak into the towel as it thaws, then toss the basil into a soup or a salad.

Pesto is another nice find in your winter freezer. Mix 1 cup basil, ¼ cup olive oil, 2 tbsp. pine nuts or almonds chopped, 2 cloves garlic, crushed, ½ cup parsley, salt to taste. Freeze the pesto in small containers to use on fettuccine.

Another trick is to use zucchini as a base. Put a chunk of zucchini in the food processor to make about one cup, then toss in a cup of chopped basil, oregano or whatever herb you want to preserve. Freeze in containers and pop the whole mix into your winter soup.

Freezing parsley is no trouble at all. Wash it and toss into a bag. Whatever you save now will become as precious as gold when you are cooking next winter and longing for the taste of something green.

A Canadian couple travelling in Ireland were ordering a meal in a pub and he said "No potatoes." Every person in the room stopped eating and stared at him. The waitress refused to take him seriously. His wife couldn't stand the pressure. She said, "Order potatoes!"
As if to make up for his temporary aberration, the waitress brought him an enormous plate-full.

Digging potatoes at Hillview Farm

Some autumn night your
garden will be visited by frost
and summer will be over.

Tomatoes provide vitamin A and C and some iron. They also contain lycopene, a type of carotene which may not be good for people with arthritis.

Onions are believed to be powerful antioxidants. They contain vitamins A, B, C, calcium, magnesium, phosphorus, sulphur, potassium, sodium, iron, zinc, iodine, silicon, phosphoric acids, and citrate of lime.

TOMATO - ONION CASSEROLE

**10 small tomatoes (plum are nice),
or a 15 oz. can
5 medium onions cut in half
1½ cups soft bread crumbs
3 tbsp. butter
1 tbsp. each of chopped basil, oregano, parsley
1/8 tsp. onion salt or powdered garlic**

Arrange tomatoes in casserole with half onion between each one. Sprinkle with salt or garlic and herbs. Melt butter in frying pan on stove; stir in crumbs and spoon on top allowing veggies to peek through. Bake at 190°C (375°F) for 20-25 minutes.

A red wagon enables easy moving of container plants in and out of a garage when frost threatens.

Ground cherries growing in a garden at Maniwaki, Quebec (zone 3). The fruit can be used to make jam or pies.

Cucumbers supply vitamins A, C, calcium and some iron. Made into relish, they add zest to any winter meal.

LILY LAKE HOT-DOG RELISH

This recipe was passed up and down our road in the 1960s. I've been making it every summer since and when children phone from distant cities, they ask if I have made it yet this year. Don't start doing this one unless you are prepared for a long commitment.

14 cucumbers (not peeled)
10 onions
2 red peppers
2 green peppers
$1/3$ cup salt
6 cups white sugar
1 cup flour
2 tbsp. dry mustard
1 tbsp. turmeric
2 tsp. celery seed
4 cups vinegar
1 cup water

Chop vegetables. Put salt on top. Leave overnight. Drain. Mix remaining ingredients and boil for 5 minutes, then add relish. Cook 10 minutes more. Stir constantly because this tends to stick. Pack in sterilized jars.

> Diary, Sept. 16: Outdoors the days are mellow, golden and still. There's a temptation to linger doing nothing, to imbibe September as it is. There's also the urgency remembered from a more primitive past to save some of it, to stash it away against the coming winter.
> So indoors there are herbs hanging to dry and vegetables to be frozen and the very essence of September - chili sauce bubbling on the stove sending sweet and tangy smells throughout the house.

Ethel Roe mentioned in Country magazine that she could make microwave pickles in just four hours. The magazine had so many requests for her recipe that she prepared a little booklet of her favourite microwave recipes and sent them to lucky people like me. Here is:

ETHEL ROE'S MICROWAVE PICKLES

6 medium cucumbers
2 medium onions (optional)
½ cup salt
2 quarts water
1 cup vinegar
1 cup water
2 cups vinegar
1 cup hot tap water
1 cup white sugar
1 cup light brown sugar (packed)
½ tsp. mustard seed
½ tsp. celery seed
½ tsp. turmeric

Slice cucumbers and onions in large mixing bowl. Sprinkle with salt. Add 2 quarts water, cover with ice cubes and let stand 2 to 3 hours. Drain completely and rinse. Place slices in 2 quart casserole. Add 1 cup each water and vinegar. Cover. Place in microwave on high for 10 minutes, stirring after 5 minutes. Drain well discarding the liquid. In 3 quart casserole mix the remaining ingredients. Cover. Place in microwave and cook 6 minutes. Add cucumbers and return to microwave. Cook on high for 11-13 minutes. Pack into sterilized jars and seal. Let stand at least 24 hours before serving.

Pumpkin fun

CHAPTER 10

OCTOBER

HAULING IN THE HARVEST

"We don't inherit our resources from our parents and grandparents. We borrow from our children and grandchildren."

Bud Wildman [1]

Prolonging your garden in fall is an interesting game so long as you don't mind losing. Whatever you do, Old Man Frost is going to reach down one still, starlit night and freeze your carefully mulched and blanketed beauties anyway.

If you have watched and worried and covered and uncovered until you are tired of the game, it is time to gather in your harvest. There is a great satisfaction in piling a wheelbarrow or wagon full of turnips or squash or potatoes and hauling it toward the house.

Now that the wheelbarrow is loaded with vegetables, where are we going to put this stuff? Ideal storage conditions vary for different vegetables but a root cellar will take care of most of them. The traditional root cellar was dug into the side of a hill preferably not too far from the house. The purpose of a root cellar is access to a place below the frost level where temperature remains constant a few degrees above freezing. To know what is going on in your root cellar, you will need a thermometer to measure temperature and a **hygrometer** or humidity gauge to measure humidity.

If your root cellar is not cold enough in early winter you will need to admit cool night air through a louvred ventilator or an exhaust pipe. If it gets too cold in winter, more insulation is needed - Styrofoam on the door, sawdust, wood shavings, straw or leaves packed around the vegetables.

A humidity of 90% is ideal for root vegetables. If your root cellar lacks humidity you can pack vegetables in damp sand or sawdust and/or reduce ventilation air flow. Good ventilation will likely ensure against too much humidity. Both an air intake pipe and an outlet pipe are necessary to allow air to circulate; cool air comes in the low intake pipe and warm air makes its exit through the higher pipe.

A harvest of squash ready for winter storage in the basement.

If you are not ready to dig a root house into your hillside or you have no hillside, there are other places where you can store vegetables. An older house may offer a basement with a dirt floor which gives you good humidity and cool temperature. A newer house is more challenging. You might be able to partition off a room against a north wall by insulating all but the cold north wall. The space under a porch can be made into an effective root cellar. Some people use outside window wells by lining the bottom with hardware cloth to keep out mice, then putting down alternate layers of straw and vegetables, ending with straw. Cover with a board and plastic to keep out water. Open your basement window to reach into this magic larder.

If that wheelbarrow full of vegetables has no other destination try the garage. Carrots, turnips, beets, potatoes will likely be safe here until Christmas in zones 5 or higher. You can add protection by heaping bags of leaves on top of your containers or packing the vegetables in sawdust or leaves. By January we will need to bring the remaining vegetables indoors. A simple and easily accessible storage place in your home could be a spare bedroom with the heat turned off or a closet against a north wall.

One year an early cold snap froze a bushel of apples in our garage. I put frozen apples into a 9x12 inch baking dish, poured ¾ cup maple syrup over the lot and baked them at 205°C (400°F). When partly cooked I removed cores with an apple-corer and put in cinnamon, brown sugar and a dab of butter. The apples stayed frozen in the garage and I used them for two months in this way.

Not all vegetables want to be kept cold and damp. Winter squash and pumpkins like temperatures of 10-15°C (50-60°F) with 60-70% humidity. Most basements can provide a corner, not close to the furnace, with temperatures in this range. Onions and garlic and dried beans like a combination of cool temperature, just above freezing, with low humidity.

Pumpkins are a special joy in October. Their colour is right; they sit like harvest moons in the garden. They are round and fat and funny, made for Hallowe'en. Small children love seeing them grow so fast, watching their vines reach across the lawn, seeing the fruit turn from pale green to bright orange. Growing a giant pumpkin can be fun. In contrast to the sweet little pie pumpkins, monsters like Hundred Weight or Atlantic Giant can weigh in at 100 kilograms.

Children are good harvesters. They understand that these toys are real. Anna, aged one-and-a-half, had fun picking pumpkins. But when her father cut the top off one to make a Jack-o-lantern and began to dig out the pulp, she burst into tears. It seems likely that the pumpkin had become her friend.

When harvesting, leave some stem on the pumpkin. Let it cure on a warm lawn to harden the skin. Store both squash and pumpkin at 10-16°C (50-60°F). Thousands of pumpkins won't make it past Hallowe'en but their seeds can be roasted and used as a nutritious snack (B vitamins, zinc and calcium). After they have sagged on the porch they will make wonderful compost. But don't hurry Jack away - even a dilapidated post-Hallowe'en pumpkin with sagging expression and a cap of snow can be fun for kids.

Hauling up the giant pumpkin

By the end of October some of us are cooking squash or tiny pie pumpkins every time the oven is on. I put the whole squash in the microwave for five minutes to make the skin soft enough to cut it in half. Then I remove the seeds, put the halves upside down in a 9x12 inch baking dish with one inch of water and cook at 205°C (400°F) until soft. Now the skin and its contents part company easily. The squash can be mashed or put into a food processor. Sometimes, to win over those who don't like squash, I add ¼ cup milk, 1 to 2 tbsp. butter, 1 tsp. cinnamon, ½ tsp. ginger, brown sugar and salt to taste.

In October squash are so sweet that you may need none of this. Because we use it regularly all winter, I freeze mashed squash in casserole dishes or freezer containers or slide solid chunks into freezer bags to be mashed up later.

Hillview Organic Farm

Tiny sweet pie pumpkins can be cooked up whenever the oven is in use, then mashed or blended to wait in refrigerator or freezer until you want to make pumpkin pie. Pumpkin and squash also make wonderful soup. Either one can be used for muffins or loaf cake or cheesecake.

In several cities across Canada people with no garden of their own have the opportunity to get a basket of garden-fresh organic-grown produce delivered to their door every week. It's called Community Shared Agriculture (CSA). Farmers grow abundant vegetables and deliver them to people who pay a flat fee once a year. It's a plan which allows direct contact between farmer and consumer, which eliminates the middle man and the high fuel consumption of long-distance cartage. In order to market produce as organic, farmers have to meet a set of standards which ensure that the food is grown without pesticides or chemical fertilizers in soil kept fertile with manure and compost, mulch and crop rotation. When Joan and John Smith of Hillview Organic Farm at Warsaw, Ont. started their CSA operation in 1990, it was the second such venture in Ontario. When Dan and Wilma Wiens of St. Adolphe, Man., started the first CSA venture on the prairies in 1992, media coverage resulted in 200 shareholders signing up within one day. Now the idea, which

Pumpkin Harvest

Pumpkins in the morning mist near Sidney on Vancouver Island

originated in Japan, has spread all across Canada with names like Sunset Garden near Bramber, NS, La Généreuse near Sherbrooke, PQ, and Simple Abundance near Winnipeg, MN.

An important aspect of CSA gardening is the social bond between producer and consumer. Families who sign up understand that they are "sharing the risk" along with the farmer. Crops are subject to drought, floods or hail; families will eat what the land produces and this will vary from year to year.

But families share more than the risk. They are usually welcome to visit the farm and sometimes they share the work. Pot-luck get-togethers and harvest festivals let producer and consumer become a true community while they share wholesome fun. Lofstedt Farm at Kaslo, B.C., hosts three annual festivals - at Easter, St. John's and Michaelmas. La Généreuse has a Fête des Fleurs in springtime, Harvest Day in August and sleigh rides in winter.

No two CSAs are alike. Most consist of private farms selling shares to city dwellers and delivering food to them. Some consist of a co-op group which leases land and hires a farmer to grow the vegetables. Harvest Share Co-op near Fredericton works this way. In Alberta growers and sharers cobbled together eight farms and 130 shareholders to start a CSA operation near Calgary.

Some operations involve direct door-to-door delivery - a box of fresh in-season vegetables brought to your doorstep by the people who grow it. In Calgary members pick up their baskets of vegetables at drop-off centres in the city. In Newfoundland, Cathy Young and Ted Walsh organized their operation by "doing boxes" on their farm near Markland, then driving to their house in St. John's where friends and neighbours could come to pick up their boxes of produce.

What all the CSA operations have in common is providing fresh, organic food directly from farm to family table. Farmer-gardeners have the satisfaction of personally knowing the families they are feeding. Shareholders express satisfaction in having tasty, chemical-free food and supporting local farmers while protecting the environment.

A small section of organic produce can now be found in most supermarkets, its quality steadily improving.

During summer, roadside stands may offer fresh organic vegetables. At farmers' markets in many cities there are stalls with "organic" signs. You can talk directly to the farmer/gardener about how the food is grown and he or she can talk to you about what you want next week or next year. It's a good relationship.

To prolong the tomato season pull up the plants and move them into the garage. The fruit will ripen slowly for another month.

Diary, Oct. 28: In the week before Halloween there comes one warm still day, a gift for gardeners who have not finished outdoor tasks. I use it to pull root vegetables and dig potatoes and cut the stalks of peonies and phlox. Rampant growth of tansy and mint and oregano is chopped off and added still green to the compost heap. Its bulk will loosen and aerate the heap and its green will promote a little action when mixed with brown leaves. A bag of manure and earth from patio containers sprinkled on the layers contributes microorganisms. I cover the pile with straw or leaves to prevent leaching when it rains, and a few heavy branches to hold it together when the wind blows. This will be a slow cooker compost pile gradually breaking down over winter. Then I move the black compost bin to sit just outside the garage door so I don't need to visit the big compost pile with kitchen peelings when it's 40° below. OK snow, we're ready!

Pumpkin's beta carotene content is very high. It also supplies vitamin A and potassium. Pumpkins and squash can be interchanged in most recipes. Use either to make pies, cakes, muffins, cookies, breads, soups, and casseroles.

PUMPKIN PIE
1½ cups brown sugar
1 tsp. cinnamon
½ tsp. salt
½ tsp. ginger
3 eggs
3 cups pumpkin
1 cup milk
1 cup cream
Mix first six ingredients in the order given. Scald the milk and cream by heating on stove or in microwave; add to pumpkin mixture. Pour pumpkin mixture into two uncooked pie crusts. Sprinkle nutmeg on top.
Bake at 220°C (425°F) for 15 minutes,
Reduce heat to 180°C (350°F) until pie is firm and a knife inserted in centre comes out clean.

ROASTED VEGETABLES
carrots and parsnips (pre-cook in water 5 min.)
yams, celery root, onions turnip (cook 3 min. in microwave to make peeling easier)
Chop all vegetables into pieces about 1x2 in. Toss in olive oil. Sprinkle generously with Herbes de Provence mixture (Recipe on p. 69). Roast at 205°C (400°F) covered 20 minutes, then uncovered 20 minutes.
Roast beets separately after tossing in balsamic or wine vinegar plus a little olive oil plus Herbes de Provence.

The squash family includes this ornamental gourd.

Soup simmers on the stove.

CHAPTER 11

NOVEMBER

THE MOON OF SOUP

There is something magical and curative about the powers of nature as seen in the growth of a plant.
Mitchell L. Hewson [1]

November is synonymous with dry, dark, drear, depressed. Frost has turned the garden black, the lawn brown, the trees stark and bare. The best we can hope for is four months of snow. If ever anyone needed comfort food it is a Canadian in November. Perhaps that's why I have overheard people lately in grocery stores and bank line-ups discussing what they put in their home-made soup.

Making soup is one of the best ways to ward off the cold and the dark. It is also a good way to store some of the abundant harvest just gathered in. What your family can't eat you can freeze in containers for late-winter eating.

Soups come in as many shapes and colours as the cook's imagination. They can be cold soups in summertime but in November they had better be hot. They can be creamed or clear broth or chowders or hearty bean and ham concoctions. But the soup I keep hearing about when I'm out shopping is the once-around-the-garden vegetable soup made with or without meat stock.

Stock is the soup base made by simmering beef or chicken bones in a big pot for three to four hours. A few stalks of celery with leafy tops, two onions and one or two leeks can be added for flavour and later discarded. When stock is cooked remove bones and vegetables and strain the stock through a sieve. Put stock in a cold place to set so that the fat can be lifted off the top. Your stock is now ready to make soup; or it can go into the freezer for making soup later.

What to put in your soup depends entirely on what you have. My notebooks say: Thanksgiving Soup, Oct. 13, still had fresh from the garden: beans, carrots, kohlrabi, cabbage, tomatoes. By November we're dependent mainly on our harvested store but the garden may still yield kale and parsley and carrots tucked under their leafy counterpanes.

My list of candidates for vegetable soup:
stock (3 cups)
water (3 cups)
tomatoes (fresh if available or canned)
cabbage
zucchini
green pepper
onions (green onion tops too)
celery
yellow beans
carrots
kohlrabi
spinach
broccoli
potatoes
squash
turnips
rice
macaroni
dried peas or beans (soak peas or beans overnight using 3 cups of water. Or boil 2 minutes, let stand 1 hour.)
oregano
basil
celery seed
thyme
salt, pepper
2 garlic cloves crushed

If you lack stock and gravy you can buy soup bases (bulk food stores have a base without monosodium glutamate to which many people are allergic). Other nice soup additions from the bulk food store are chick pea base, onion soup base and bean flour.

There are many short cuts to making soup. When I have gravy left over from a Sunday roast, often it forms the base of a Monday soup. With luck I have saved the

Falling leaves

Diary, Nov. 3: Raking leaves is a more satisfying occupation when the leaves are worth their weight in gold for your winter compost pile. There is still some green in the Norway maple leaves coming down but the hard maple, birch and mountain ash leaves are brown. This brown can be layered with the green of container geraniums and lobelia thrown on the pile, the bulky remains of tansy and turnip greens and cauliflower and broccoli plants.

If you have an abundance of leaves, run over them with your lawn mower to reduce their bulk, bag them in strong garbage bags and store in a shed or outside under some shrubs. When you open the bags in the spring there will be sweet and spicy brown material to balance the green in your compost.

water from potatoes and some other cooked vegetables. Sometimes there is leftover spaghetti sauce or V-8 juice in the refrigerator to add to the pot. If you like lentils in soup, a can of black beans or pinto beans or even pork n' beans can add a lot of taste with no fuss. A spoonful of salsa added to a pot of soup can give it a nice flavour. Chopping vegetables is not time-consuming when you can throw them all in a food processor. Soup can easily be a half-hour affair.

Cooking soup is like burning wood. Thoreau said wood warms you twice, once in the work of chopping it, once in the burning. Vegetable soup warms you in the work of growing the vegetables, in the cooking and again in the eating.

Gardening as therapy, as a way to warm our hearts and energize our bodies is being explored by health centres in many cities. In Abbotsford, B.C., the Regional Psychiatric Centre for long-time offenders uses horticulture as a form of therapy. In Montreal, patients in an AIDS centre have become award-winning gardeners and claim that they are living longer because of their interest in gardening. In Toronto, the Hugh MacMillan Rehabilitation Centre uses their Spiral Garden to help children regain skills for living. Special raised beds allow them to work from wheel chairs. By adopting a plant or tree, caring for it and studying everything that happens to it, wounded children can turn their attention and creativity outward again.

Retirement homes in many cities are using gardens to combat the feeling of uselessness that often overcomes the elderly. Twice a year Bob and Irene Williamson help the residents at Rest Haven Lodge in Sidney, British Columbia to plant hanging baskets. "In early April/May we assemble a team of volunteers and staff and with hundreds of tiny plants, the residents get their

Raised beds for people with limited mobility.

hands into the peat moss planting medium and proceed to create a dozen or more summer time baskets and half a dozen planter pots. Despite my worst fears about the sometimes none too gentle treatment that those tiny specimens receive, by mid June, we inevitably end up with truly vibrant, colourful baskets which brighten the outdoor areas through until about early October. By then it is time to say good bye to the summer plants and repeat the process with winter pansies which normally last until the end of March." Working together gives these residents new purpose, focuses social life, adds a little fun and provides year-round enjoyment of the beauty and fragrance they helped to create.

In Peterborough last summer homeowners offered their back yards to the Association of People with Head Injuries so that patients could experience growing vegetables and flowers.

Kathleen Yeomans in her book, *The Able Gardener - Overcoming Barriers of Age and Physical Limitation*s, discusses raised beds, adaptive devices, easy to access containers. An occupational and physical therapist, she promotes gardening adapted for disabled or age-stiffened gardeners.

Mitchell Hewson, working at the Homewood Health Centre in Guelph, Ontario, has seen the power of plants in programs of therapy and rehabilitation. People with schizophrenia, depression, Alzheimer's, anorexia nervosa and alcohol and drug addiction have benefited physically, emotionally, socially and spiritually by working in the greenhouses and out-of-doors in the 47 acres of garden and bush at Homewood.

In his book, *Horticulture as Therapy,*[1] Mitchell Hewson tells how plants heal individual clients. "A man in his early forties was admitted with a diagnosis of alcohol dependency. Because of his alcohol abuse he had patterns of instability in his job and family relationships. When working in the greenhouse, he was surprised to see the effect of over-watered plants, especially a large jade plant. The plant was becoming very yellow and sickly. He made the connection, realizing the same thing was happening to him because of his disease process. It was this symbiotic relationship that helped him to acknowledge his alcohol addiction. The client went on to acquire good skills in horticulture, particularly in landscaping. Since discharge, he has changed his life style, using his leisure time for gardening and neighbourhood landscaping. Follow-up has shown that he now has a stable work pattern and stronger bonds with his family."

Mitchell Hewson, a registered horticultural-therapist-masters, has worked for 25 years at Homewood Health Centre where he initiated the first horticultural therapy program in Canada in 1973. He is a founding member of the Canadian Horticultural Therapy Association which gives workshops and seminars across the country for recreational and occupational therapists, nurses, educators and others who work in health-care facilities, helping them discover the power of plants as healing tools.

Newspaper reports on men arrested in North America for Nazi war crimes describe them as avid gardeners. Is it possible that these men were attempting to heal themselves of terrible things seen and done in their dreadful past? Were they attempting through contact with the earth, air and water to regain some goodness they had once known in their early lives?

In everyday life there are reports of people who "just feel better" when they garden. Aches and pains disappear (unless you overdo the digging that first week in May). People say that their blood pressure goes down, strength and energy levels improve. Those, like me, who get themselves too busy, can find a garden recreative. I have an uneasy relationship with time. My bad dreams feature time, being late, running out of time, having to do more than is possible in a set period of time. While doing housework I watch the clock and worry about getting things done in time for whatever. But when I go outside and work in the garden time dissolves away. I go out for an hour and stay for three or four and it doesn't matter. When I go back inside I get the necessary things done in less time or see what does not need doing.

Doreen Gokiert works from her wheel chair
to create a hanging basket.

A friend of mine lost her 23-year-old daughter to leukemia in May. To get through the grief this mother turned to gardening creating Nancy's Garden using lily-of-the-valley Nancy had given her for Mother's Day and plants brought to Nancy before she died and given to the family afterward in her memory. "I believe thoroughly in the therapeutic and healing power of gardening," says Nancy's mother. "The garden got me through my first summer, and still does. I am out there a lot because I collect the flowers to dry and press and it's so peaceful there. It is the only place I am consistently at peace."

Something is happening here that has to do with more than the colour of the roses or the size of the turnips. It has to do with the healing power of nature, the sense of well-being produced by a complex array of exercise, sunshine, wind, outdoor sounds, fresh air, perhaps the rekindled memories of long hours of childhood play. All these factors may trigger the release of endorphins, chemicals in the brain which provide a sense of well-being.

Many gardeners suspect there is a great deal more going on in a garden than anyone knows. Dr. Beresford-Kroeger, a former heart research scientist with a background in botany, biochemistry and organic and nuclear chemistry, is now devoting her time to researching thousands of plant species in her garden near Ottawa. She lectures in universities, educates children and generally spreads the word about the importance of gardens to the survival of the human race. She says that just brushing against a flowering bergamot (Monarda didyma or Monarda fistulosa) releases alkaloids from the leaf surface which are good for lung ailments. What else may be happening when we brush against mint or borage or rosemary? We catch a small glimpse of what a garden has to offer in the current popularity of certain plants: feverfew to give relief from migraine headaches, valerian to help sleeplessness and purple cone flower (echinacea) to boost the immune system when cold or flu threatens.

Many of the discoveries we make in the next decade will not be new at all but rediscoveries of plants used by natives of North and South America or by ancient peoples in Africa or Asia.

Hanging basket planted by residents of Rest Haven Lodge
in Sidney, British Columbia.

Winter in Canada can catch a garden or an apple tree by surprise.

CARROT PEA SOUP

1 can cream of chicken soup
1 can pea soup (28 oz.)
1 cup cream
1½ cups milk
1 cup sliced carrots cooked five minutes
2 tbsp. chopped onion
¼ tsp. black pepper
¼ tsp. ground thyme

In a food processor blend the soups, then add the milk and cream, then remaining ingredients. Heat in a large bowl in a microwave. If heating on a stove stir often as this soup tends to stick.

SASKATOON SOUP

1 pound ground beef   2 medium potatoes
1 onion   1 cup carrots
½ cup celery   2 tsp. salt
½ green pepper   2 tbsp. sugar
4 cups hot water   ¼ tsp. pepper
3 tbsp. parsley
1 large can tomatoes (28 oz.)
2 cans tomato paste (5½ oz.)
6-7 cups cabbage, coarsely chopped

Chop vegetables. Sauté beef, onion, celery, pepper. Add rest of ingredients except cabbage. Simmer uncovered one hour, stirring occasionally. Add cabbage and simmer one more hour. If too thick add hot water.

107

First snow on patio plants.

CHAPTER 12

DECEMBER

THE SLEEPING GARDEN

The true harvest of my daily life is somewhat as intangible and indescribable as the tints of morning or evening. It is a little stardust caught, a segment of the rainbow which I have clutched... .

Thoreau [1]

While the garden sleeps under a blanket of snow the gardener dreams. December is a busy month so the dreaming is likely to come at the end of it after the turkey and the turnip casserole have been eaten on the 25th. Then it will be time to sit by a roaring fire and read our new garden books or admire the shiny new toys we will put to work in the garden, come spring.

Early in December when shopping for Christmas, it is sometimes difficult to get our minds past snow shovels and skis. But on Dec. 22 the days start to lengthen and it is only three months until you can go out and dig the parsnips. Seed catalogues arrive in the mail in early December, some with pages of gift ideas (See list on page 111).

T & T Seeds from Winnipeg caters to a short growing season (they'll supply you with cantaloupe designed to ripen at the end of August). They have pages of baskets, containers, trays, planters, shelves, growing lights, seed sowers, soil amenders, slug-pits,

bird feeders, pruners and snippers, sandals with nails that aerate your lawn, a kit to build a fountain in your back yard, phosphate-free shampoo, vitamins and herbal supplements. Most but not all of their problem-solvers are organic.

Stokes offers compost catchers, watering cans, hammocks, books, easy-kneeler stools, tool-carrying kits, pot holders to fit over a mailbox, even a kit to build a greenhouse and a bird bath with a heater.

Gardening calendars are a welcome gift for anyone with a green thumb. They come with tips and reminders and folklore suitable to the month. Gardening books are a must for the garden-dreamer. Whatever the grower's particular interest, from herbs to roses to cabbages, there will be a book to tell you how. Gardening magazines are a gift that arrives several times during the year. Children's books about growing things will introduce your little ones to some of the magic in the garden and the natural world around it.

You might consider fashion when shopping for Christmas. Most gardening friends have a wardrobe that could stand sprucing up. Quite often the resident scarecrow makes a better fashion statement than the gardener.

Practicality comes first for every serious digger in the earth. In the spring when you spread the 'm' word on your garden (and for some time afterward) you want to be covered in old clothes. I keep a change of clothes in the laundry entrance room, discard my dirty ones when I come in for lunch and put them on again when I go back out.

If you have a really comfortable pair of shoes no longer nice enough for the house, designate them "garden shoes". There is no rule that your shoes have to look good but they do have to be sturdy to push that spade and tote that load. Duck boots by the back door are excellent for stepping into and for keeping feet dry in rainy weather.

Unless you garden in the dark a big hat is de rigueur. Straw is great because it lets the breeze in while keeping out the ultraviolet rays. It should be big enough to protect not only head and face but shoulders and arms when you kneel to weed. Some garden hats are beautiful - an opportunity here for a fashion statement. Personally I have yet to find one that is beautiful and stays on my head - an opportunity here for some designer to get it right.

While shorts and halter tops look good on magazine covers, long hours in the garden require long pants and shirts with long sleeves and high necks to avoid too much sun (light colours are good for coolness).

The finishing touch for the well-dressed gardener is the gloves. These can be a riot of flowers or simply elegant. I prefer simply elegant since they will soon be

The resident scarecrow sometimes makes a better fashion statement than the gardener.

Joan Rawlinson's herb vinegar on display at a community garden harvest party.

covered with mud. The important thing is the stitching: pay more and get good stitching so the thumbs and fingers won't wear out in a week. There is nothing worse than a glove that doesn't keep out the dirt. If you give a friend good ones for Christmas, she or he will bless you all summer long.

There are two kinds of garden gifts: those like the gloves and hat and duck boots and tools that will find their way outside to the garden; and those that come in from the garden. Some of these look beautiful under a Christmas tree - mint jelly, crabapple jelly, strawberry jam, herb vinegars, antipasto, pickles, cucumber relish or chili sauce, pesto, zucchini bread, carrot cake.

Herbs can be dried and packaged or bottled as gifts or you can present them as ornamental wreaths or swags or basket arrangements. Oregano picked in late summer and hung in bundles to dry, will keep its deep purple colour. Use a small grapevine wreath as your base and fill it with oregano. Add a white lacy bow and you have a tasty and pretty kitchen wreath.

To make a swag lay two bundles of oregano facing opposite directions but with stems that overlap about five inches. Add other dried collectables to each bundle - poppy heads, love-in-a-mist, lavender, tansy, statice, the pink plumes of smoke bush, baby's breath, whatever decorative possibilities you collected from your garden on those golden days of August and September and hung in an airy room to dry.

To create a Christmas arrangement which will last several weeks, snip cedars and junipers and pine and put into wet oasis in a plastic-lined basket. Add the red berries of swamp holly or bittersweet or the heads of love-in-a-mist or poppies. Add pine cones and a red bow.

Now in December with the decorations made, it is awfully nice in the chair by the fire. But if you do want to go outside, there are carrots to be found out there under their 20 inches of leaves. I carry a pail of warm water with me when I go out to dig December carrots. I can break off the tops and swish the carrots around in the warm water without freezing my hands. These fresh carrots will taste three times as good as the ones you buy in the store.

While you are in the garden, pick the kale - those bright green leaves poking through the snow. Kale is planted early in August which probably explains its absence in most gardens. It is hard to remember to plant in August. One way is to keep kale in mind as a replacement for the row of heat-damaged lettuce or the worn-out beans you want to pull out in midsummer. Kale's dark green curly leaves are beautiful enough to give it room in the garden or make it a centrepiece on your table even if you never eat it.

But eating it is a good idea for most people. The National Academy of Sciences report, "Diet, Nutrition and Cancer," recommends vitamins A, C, E and selenium for cancer prevention and heart protection. Kale is high in all of these. It is very high in calcium and also has riboflavin, niacin, magnesium, iron, sulphur, sodium, potassium, phosphorus and chlorophyll. (Persons taking anticoagulants should know that kale's vitamin K might promote blood clotting.) Kale's flavour is improved by frost which changes the plant's metabolism and makes it sweeter.

Recipes for cooking kale are not very evident in the average cookbook. You may have to improvise. Begin by substituting kale in recipes that call for spinach or even eggplant. Instead of spinach pie you can make kale pie. Instead of eggplant with spaghetti sauce and parmesan cheese, try kale. It is good in soup or you can steam it like spinach and dress it up with lemon juice and butter when you want quick-and-easy. My favourite way to use it is the Irish way, chopped up and added to mashed potatoes.

There may be another vegetable you can pick from your December garden - winter lettuce. Planted where the most heat is available, possibly by a south-facing brick wall, winter lettuce can be grown and protected by row covers during cold spells to extend the season to Christmas even in zone five.

Choose varieties bred for winter hardiness. Plant in late summer if trying for a long fall harvest. Plant in early fall for very early picking next spring. Look for Boston-type lettuces like Winter Marvel, Bronze Winter, Arctic King or North Pole. Winter Density is a hardy semi-romaine. Arugula is a cold-tolerant tangy tasting lettuce that adds zip to mixed salad. For loose-leaf lettuce, try Black Seeded Simpson.

Back in the house it is time to do the turnip casserole. Turnips or rutabagas are easy to grow. They need 50 to 100 days depending on variety. Turnips are smaller, usually white with tender greens. They grow fast and can be planted in mid-summer for fall harvest. Rutabagas are larger, often yellow, and are better keepers for winter storage. Either are happy to stay outside until the ground freezes. To keep three or four months after harvest, store in sand in a cool place just above freezing.

Turnips are cruciferous with cancer-fighting substances and vitamins A and C as well as calcium, iron and niacin.

APPLE - TURNIP CASSEROLE
large turnip
$^1/_3$ cup brown sugar
1 to 2 tbsp. butter
2 apples
Topping:
¼ cup brown sugar
$^1/_3$ cup flour
1 tbsp. butter
½ tsp. cinnamon
½ tsp. cloves

Put turnip in microwave on high 5 minutes to make peeling easier. Dice. Boil until cooked. Drain. Add butter and mash. Peel apples. Slice. Toss in the brown sugar and spices. Layer in casserole: turnip, then apple slices. Repeat then top with turnip. For topping, mix together brown sugar and flour. Cut in butter. Sprinkle on casserole. Bake at 180°C (350°F) 1 hour.

KALE - POTATO SOUP
1 onion, chopped
3 cups chicken stock (or use soup base powder)
1 cup leeks, chopped (white part)
1½ cups peeled potatoes, chopped
2 cups kale, chopped
1 cup milk (or soy milk)
salt and pepper
fresh dill or parsley

Simmer chicken stock, onions, leeks, potatoes about 20-30 minutes. Add kale. Cook about 5 minutes. Add milk, salt and pepper. Add dill or parsley to individual servings.

RED AND GREEN VEGGIE DIP
8 oz. cream cheese
1 tomato, peeled and finely chopped
1 tsp. onion, chopped or grated
1 tsp. parsely, chopped
½ tsp. salt
1 to 2 drops Tabasco sauce

Blend cream cheese and tomato using fork. Add other ingredients and chill.

ORANGE - ALMOND WINTER SALAD
11 oz. can mandarin oranges
3 cups winter lettuce
½ red onion, sliced
½ cup slivered almonds, toasted
Dressing: shake in a jar and chill before serving,
½ cup salad oil

3 tbsp. wine vinegar	1 to 1½ tbsp. sugar
1 tbsp. lemon juice	½ tsp. salt
½ tsp. grated onion	½ tsp. dry mustard

Turnips

Oregano, poppies, love-in-a-mist and globe thistle gathered in early September can be hung in a dimly-lit airy room, then used in arrangements and wreaths and swags.

114

Canadian Seed Catalogues supplying vegetables and herbs. Many offer free catalogues, others charge as noted by $.

Aimers
81 Temperance St.
Aurora, ON L4G 2R1 $

Alberta Nurseries & Seeds Ltd.
P.O. Box 20
Bowden, AB T0M 0K0

Ken Allen Seeds
536 MacDonnell St.
Kingston, ON K7K 4W7

Aurora Farm
RR 1, 63-9
Creston, BC V0B 1G0
untreated seeds $

Dacha Barinka
46232 Strathcona Road
Chilliwack, BC V2P 3T2

William Dam Seeds Ltd.
Box 8400
Dundas, ON L9H 6M1 $

Dominion Seed House
Box 2500
Georgetown, ON L7G 5L6

Early's Farm & Garden Centre
2615 Lorne Ave.
Saskatoon, SK S7J 0S5

Ecogenesis Seeds
16 Jedburgh Road
Toronto, ON M5M 3J6
untreated seeds $

Halifax Seed Company
P.O. Box 8026, Stn.A.
Halifax, NS B3K 5L8

Happy Herbs
RR 2
Uxbridge, ON L96 1R2 $

The Herb Farm
RR4
Norton, NB E0G 2N0
untreated seeds $

Heritage Seed Program
RR 2
Uxbridge, NB L9P 1R3
membership fee

Holes Greenhouses & Garden Ltd.
101 Bellerose Dr.
St. Albert, AB T8N 8N8 $

Island Seed Co. Ltd.
P.O. Box 4278, Depot 3
Victoria, BC V8X 3X8 $

Lindenberg Seeds Ltd.
803 Princess Ave.
Brandon, MB R7A 0P5

Manhattan Farms Ltd.
3088 Salmon River Road
Salmon Arm, BC V1E 4M1
untreated seeds $

McFayden Seeds Ltd.
30 9th St., Suite 200
Brandon, MB R7A 6N4

Nature's Garden Seed Co.
Box 40121, 905 Garden St.
Victoria, BC V8W 3N3

Ontario Seed Company
P.O. Box 7, 330 Phillip St.
Waterloo, ON, N2J 3Z9

Prairie Grown Garden Seeds
Box 118
Cochin, SK S0M 0L0
untreated seeds

Rawlinson Garden Seed
269 College Road
Truro, NS B2N 2P6
untreated seeds

Richters
357 Hwy. 47
Goodwood, ON L0C 1A0 $

River View Herbs
Box 92
Maitland, NS B0N 1T0

Salt Spring Seeds
Box 444
Ganges, BC V0S 1E0
untreated seeds $

Stokes Seeds Ltd.
Box 10
St. Catharines, ON L2R 6R6

T&T Seeds Ltd.
Box 1710
Winnipeg, MB R3C 3P6

Territorial Seeds Ltd.
8475 Ontario St., Unit 206
Vancouver, B.C. V5X 3E8
untreated seeds

Vecey Seeds Ltd.
York, PE C0A 1P0

American Seed Catalogues of interest to northern gardeners:

Allen, Sterling & Lothrop
191 U.S. Route #1
Falmouth, ME 04105 $

The Cook's Garden
Box 535
Londonderry, VT 05148
untreated seeds

Harris Seeds
Box 22960
Rochester, NY 14692

Johnny's Selected Seeds
310 Foss Hill Rd.
Albion, ME 04910

Pinetree Garden Seeds
Box 300
New Gloucester, ME 04260

NOTES

Introduction
1. Traill, Catharine Parr, *Canadian Crusoes: A Tale of the Rice Lake Plains* (London: Arthur Hall, Virtue, & Co., 1859) xi.

Chapter 1
1. *Fourcois' Chemistry*. Quoted by Traill, Mrs., *Pearls and Pebbles* (Toronto: William Briggs, 1894) 235.

Chapter 2
1. Traill, C.P., *Letters from the Wife of an Emigrant Officer*, 27.
2. Jameson, Anna, *Winter Studies, Summer Rambles* (Toronto: McClelland & Stewart, 1923) 63.
3. Traill, Catharine Parr, *The Backwoods of Canada* (London: Charles Knight, 1863) 143.
4. Traill, 232-3.
5. Tivy, Louis, *Your Loving Anna: Letters from the Ontario Frontier* (Toronto: University of Toronto Press, 1972) 48-49.
6. Tivy, 72.
7. Tivy, 72-74.
8. Traill, Catharine Parr, *The Backwoods of Canada*, 232.
9. Traill, 149.
10. Traill, Mrs. C.P., *Studies of Plant Life in Canada* (Ottawa: A.S. Woodburn, 1885) 2-3.

Chapter 3
1. Dueck, Cathy, *Peterborough Ecology Garden: Applied Sustainability,* (Trent University, 1991) 5.

Chapter 4
1. Jefferson, Thomas, *Notes on the State of Virginia*. 1781-1785, Query 19.

Chapter 5
1. Murray, Alexander, *The Domestic Oracle*, (London: 1826).
2. Garrett, Blanche Pownall, *A Taste of the Wild* (Toronto: James Lorimer, 1975) 32.
3. Duke, Dr. James, *Organic Gardening, Dec. 1996* (Emmaus, PA: Rodale Press) 39.

Chapter 6
1. Chambers, Douglas, *Stonyground: The Making of a Canadian Garden* (Alfred A Knopf, 1996) xix.

Chapter 8
1. Goëthe (1749-1832).

Chapter 9
1. Jefferson, Thomas, letter to Charles Willson Peale.

Chapter 10
1. Wildman, Bud, Ontario Environment and Energy Minister, at opening of Peterborough Ecology Park, July 1994.

Chapter 11
1. Hewson, Mitchell L., *Horticulture as Therapy* (Guelph, Homewood Health Centre, 1994) xii
2. Hewson, 13.

Chapter 12
1. Thoreau, Henry David, *Walden* (New York: Random House, 1937) 195.

BIBLIOGRAPHY

Balch, Phyllis A. & James F., *Prescription for Cooking and Dietary Wellness* (Greenfeld, Indiana: P.A.B. Publishing, 1993).

Bennett, Jennifer, *The Harrowsmith Northern Gardener* (Camden East, Ont: Camden House, 1982).

Beresford-Kroeger, Dr. Diana, *A North Temperate Garden: Bioplanning For the Next Millennium* (Kingston: Quarry Press, 1998).
Brown, Alice Cooke, *Early American Herb Recipes* (New York: Charles E. Tuttle Co, 1966).

Buchanan, Rita, *Vegetables* (Des Moines: Meredith Books, 1994).
Carson, Rachael, *Silent Spring* (Boston: Houghton Mifflin, 1962).
Chambers, Douglas, *Stonyground: the making of a Canadian Garden* (Toronto: Alfred A. Knopf, 1996).

Clarke, Geo. H. & Malte, M. Oscar, *Fodder and Pasture Plants* (Ottawa: Department of Agriculture, 1913).

Coleman, Eliot, *Four Season Harvest* (Camden East: Old Bridge Press, 1992).

Cox, Jeff, *How to Grow Vegetables Organically* (Emmaus, PA: Rodale Press, 1988).

Cullen, Mark & Johnson, Lorraine, *The Real Dirt* (Toronto: Penguin Books Canada, 1992).

Cullen, Mark, *A Greener Thumb* (Markham: Penguin Books Canada, 1990).

Dueck, Cathy, *Peterborough Ecology Garden: Applied Sustainability* (Trent University, 1991).

Ellis, Barbara W. and Bradley, Fern Marshall, *The Organic Gardener's Handbook of Natural Insect and Disease Control* (Emmaus, PA: Rodale Press, 1992).

Fielden, Joan & Larke, Stan, *From Garden to Table* (Toronto: McClelland and Stewart, 1976).

Gay, Kathlyn, *Cleaning Nature Naturally* (Markham: Thomas Allan & Son, 1991).

Harris, Marjorie, *Ecological Gardening* (Toronto: Random House, 1991).

Hewson, Mitchell L., *Horticulture as Therapy* (Guelph: Homewood Health Centre, 1994).

Jameson, Anna, *Winter Studies, Summer Rambles* (Toronto: McClelland & Stewart, 1923).

Kramer, J., *Natural Way to Pest-Free Gardening* (New York: Charles Scribner's and Sons, 1972).

Leopold, Aldo, *A Sand County Almanac* (New York: Oxford University Press, 1987).

Osborne, Thomas, *A Compleat Body of Husbandry* (London, 1759).

Phillips, Roger & Foy, Nicky, *Herbs* (New York: Random House, 1990).

Reimer, Jan, *The Beginner's Kitchen Garden* (New York: William Morrow and Company, 1975).

Shultz, Warren, *The Chemical-Free Lawn* (Emmaus, PA: Rodale Press, 1989).

Tivy, Louis, *Your Loving Anna: Letters from the Ontario Frontier* (Toronto: University of Toronto Press, 1972).

Traill, Catharine Parr, *Letters from the Wife of an Emigrant Officer.*

Traill, Catharine Parr, *The Backwoods of Canada* (London: Charles Knight, 1836).

Traill, Mrs. C. P., *Studies of Plant Life in Canada* (Ottawa: A. S. Woodburn, 1885).

Childrens Books:

Mallory, Laura, *Mother Nature's Magic Seed* (Peterborough, Ont: Peterborough Publishing, 1996).

Perenyi, Constance, *Growing Wild* (Pickering, Ont.: Mattacchione, 1991).

INDEX